Alexander Cluny

The American Traveller

Or, observations on the present state, culture and commerce of the British colonies in America, and the further improvements of which they are capable

Alexander Cluny

The American Traveller
Or, observations on the present state, culture and commerce of the British colonies in America, and the further improvements of which they are capable

ISBN/EAN: 9783337292324

Printed in Europe, USA, Canada, Australia, Japan

Cover: Foto ©Andreas Hilbeck / pixelio.de

More available books at **www.hansebooks.com**

THE AMERICAN TRAVELLER:

OR,

OBSERVATIONS

ON THE

PRESENT STATE, CULTURE and COMMERCE

OF THE

BRITISH COLONIES in AMERICA,

And the further IMPROVEMENTS of which they are capable;

WITH

An Account of the EXPORTS, IMPORTS and RETURNS of each Colony respectively,—and of the Numbers of BRITISH Ships and Seamen, Merchants, Traders and Manufacturers employed by all collectively:

TOGETHER WITH

The Amount of the Revenue arising to Great-Britain therefrom.

In a SERIES of LETTERS, written originally to the Right Honourable the Earl of * * * * * * * *

By an OLD and EXPERIENCED TRADER.

LONDON:

Printed for E. and C. DILLY, in the Poultry, and J. ALMON, Piccadilly.
MDCCLXIX.

CONTENTS.

Letter		Page
I, & II.	General Introduction, &c.	1
III.	Observations on Hudson's Bay,	11
IV.	Continued	17
V.	Continued	22
VI.	Continued	25
VII.	Observations on Labrador,	32
VIII.	———— on Newfoundland,	36
IX.	———— on Canada,	41
X.	———— on Nova Scotia,	51
XI.	———— on St. John's and Cape Breton,	56
XII.	———— on New England,	59
XIII.	———— on Connecticut, Rhode Island and New Hampshire,	65
XIV.	———— on New York,	73
XV.	———— on Pennsylvania,	77
XVI.	———— on Virginia and Maryland,	81
XVII.	———— on North Carolina,	87
XVIII.	———— on South Carolina,	93
XIX.	———— on Georgia,	99
XX.	———— on East Florida,	105
XXI.	———— on West Florida,	108
XXII.	Recapitulatory Remarks,	113
XXIII.	Total Amount of the American Trade, &c. &c.	121

OBSERVATIONS

ON THE

CULTURE and COMMERCE

OF THE

BRITISH COLONIES, &c.

* * *

LETTER I.

My Lord,

THE laſt Time I had the Honour of converſing with your Lordſhip, you intimated a Deſire, that I ſhould draw into one Point of View, the ſeveral Hints, which I had at different Times, taken the Liberty to ſuggeſt to your Lordſhip, on the preſent State of the *Britiſh Colonies*, and the Improvements poſſible to be made in the Culture, and Commerce of them, to their and the Mother

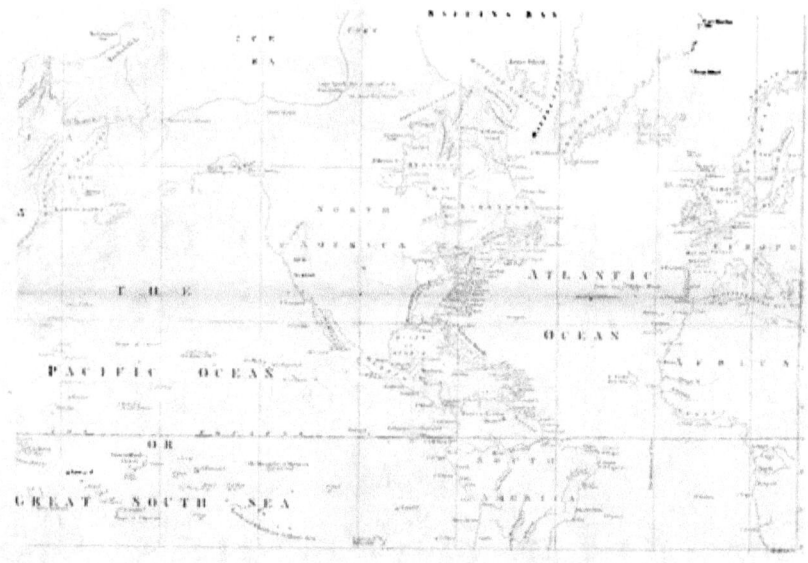

OBSERVATIONS

ON THE

CULTURE and COMMERCE

OF THE

BRITISH COLONIES, &c.

* *

LETTER I.

MY LORD,

THE laſt Time I had the Honour of converſing with your Lordſhip, you intimated a Deſire, that I ſhould draw into one Point of View, the ſeveral Hints, which I had at different Times, taken the Liberty to ſuggeſt to your Lordſhip, on the preſent State of the *Britiſh Colonies*, and the Improvements poſſible to be made in the Culture, and Commerce of them, to their and the Mother

ther Country's mutual Advantage, that you might be able with the greater Ease and Accuracy to form a Judgement yourself, and convince others of the Reality of such Advantage, and the Feasibility of the Means proposed to obtain it.

Every Intimation of your Lordship's Pleasure is a Law to me; because I know from Experience, that it is founded in Wisdom, and tends to the public Good. I shall therefore enter readily upon the Task you have prescribed, without any ostentatious Parade of diffidence in my own Abilities, (which would be an Insult to your Lordship's Judgement, rather than a Proof of my Modesty) and in the plain Words of Truth, and good Intention, lay before your Lordship those Observations, which much Experience has enabled me to make on this important Subject, together with the Facts upon which such Observations have been formed; without studying any of those Ornaments of Writing (a Study indeed, which my Life has been too closely employed in other Matters to spare Time for) that are oftenest used to gloss over a bad Cause, and mislead rather than inform the Judgement, fully sensible that your Lordship, in Things of this Nature, considers the Matter more than the Manner; and will never turn your Face away from Reason, for not being introduced in the most fashionable Dress.

In the Execution of this Attempt (for by no other Name can the Labours of any one Man to investigate a Subject of such immense Extent be properly called) I have made Choice of of this Method of conveying my Thoughts to your Lordship, in a *Series of Letters*, for several Reasons.

The first, and most applicable personally to myself, is, that having been mostly, if not solely accustomed to the epistolary Style, in a Life of Business, I can express my Thoughts more readily, and perhaps more clearly in that, than in any other. Though were not this the Case, there are abundant other Reasons to determine me to this Choice.

By this Manner of writing, I have an Opportunity of dividing my Work, so as to avoid the grievous Disadvantage of having the Reader break off, perhaps in the middle of my Argument, because he does not see a resting Place prepared for him; the most indolent, or inattentive, seldom having so little Curiosity, or being so soon tired, as to stop before they reach the End of a Letter of moderate Length.

Beside, in this Method, I may myself take the Liberty of stopping a little while, or going a few Steps out of my Way, now and then, to take Notice of any Thing that may illustrate my Subject, or enforce my own Sentiments, without Fear of giving that Offence, which might be taken at such Freedoms, in a Work of a more regular Nature; and also of recapitulating my Argument in proper Places, so as to keep it always in View, and upon Occasion collect its Force into one Point to face any Opposition.

I mention these Particulars, my Lord, not as unknown to your Lordship, but to obviate the Objection of Vanity, which may

may probably be made to my using this Mode of Writing, as if I intended to insinuate by it, a greater Intimacy with a Person of your Lordship's high Rank, and higher Character, than I really am honoured with, or ought to disclose, if I am.

In like Manner, it is my Duty to observe, that in the Course of these Letters, I shall frequently have Occasion to mention, and often to dwell upon the Proof of many Things, which are already sufficiently known to your Lordship; but this, as I said in the former Instance, is not done with the most distant Insinuation of informing you; but solely to convey that Information to others, who may not have had the same Opportunity of acquiring it; to which Knowledge I must also beg your Lordship's Pardon, and Indulgence for taking the Liberty of appealing upon many Occasions, where I apprehend that the indisputable Authority of such a Voucher may be necessary to support my own Credit.

Having thus, my Lord, given the Reasons both for my presuming to address my Thoughts on this Subject to your Lordship particularly, and in this particular Manner, I shall in my next Letter give an Account of the Matter, which I propose to submit to your Judgement, and the Method in which that Matter shall be arranged; and then proceed to obey your Lordship's Commands, without trespassing upon you with any farther Preface, or Apology.

I am with Attachment and Respect,

My Lord,
Your Lordship's most humble,
and obedient Servant.

LETTER II.

My Lord,

IT is an old Remark, that the Value of a Friend is seldom known, 'till he is lost. I most sincerely wish, this may not be the Case of *Great-Britain* with Regard to her *American Colonies*. While we went on smoothly together, we enjoyed the Advantage of our Intercourse, unequal as it was to what it might have been rendered, without ever considering the Quarter it came from, or the Means of improving, or even preserving the Continuance of it, as is too often the Case, in Respect to the greatest Blessings of Heaven.

I would not be understood to limit this Remark to either Side. It is unhappily too applicable to both. But as the first Object of every Man's Thoughts, who turns them to Matters of public Concern, is, or at least should be, the immediate Advantage of his native Country, I shall first consider how far the Colonies are advantageous to *Great-Britain*; as also how that Advantage may be still farther improved, and then the reciprocal Advantage received by the Colonies will follow of Course, and prove the mutual Interest of both to preserve that good Agreement, and Unanimity, by which alone such Advantage can be preserved; in the Discussion and Proof of which Points, the Means necessary to obtain that great End, and accomplish the many Improvements of which that Advantage is capable, will naturally, and obviously be included.

When I say, that " the first Object of a Man's Thoughts should be the Advantage of his native Country," I do not in any Sense mean that he should do, or devise any Thing unjust in itself, or injurious to the just Interest of any other Country to procure that Advantage. All I intend, is, that where the opposite Interests of his own and another Country are ballanced in the Scale of Justice, he owes a Duty to the former, which will necessarily make it preponderate in his Thoughts; a Duty of the same Nature, and derived ultimately from the same Origin, with that so strongly enforced by Reason, and Revelation, which we owe to our Parents, *the Place where*, as well as *the Persons through whom* we are called into this Life, being appointed by the Divine Giver of all Life, and consequently entitled to the same filial Attachment and Affection, though in a lesser Degree, as the Force of *Filiation*, by being centered in one Point is preserved entire, whereas that of *Patriotism* is divided perhaps between Millions, and thereby lessened on each Individual; not to insist upon the obvious Reason of the more immediate and intimate Connection in the former, than in the latter. And this shews the Error in the general Application of the antient Philosopher's saying, that he was *a Citizen of the World*, as if it implied, that all Countries ought to be equally dear to a Man of Sense, the true Meaning of it being only to inculcate *Philanthropy*, or in the sacred Style, *Good-Will towards all Mankind*; and not by any Means to deny, or invalidate

invalidate the natural, and indispensible Attachment, by which every Man is bound to his native Country.

How universal the Sense of this Attachment has ever been, and in what high Estimation the Exertion of it held, is sufficiently proved by the Honours paid to those, who have even sacrificed to it the nearest Connections of Nature, as in the Instance of the *Roman Brutus*, and the first Principle of human Action, Self-preservation, in those of the *Decii*, with many others, both *Romans* and *Athenians*, unnecessary to be enumerated here; and this among the most civilized Nations; those more ignorant carrying the Point still farther, and in the enthusiastic Ardour of their Gratitude, thinking *human Honours* too little, and therefore conferring *divine*, on such general Benefactors of Mankind.

Your Lordship will pardon this little Digression in Elucidation of a Point so dear to you, as to be made the evident Rule of your public Life, for the Necessity of it to obviate the Imputation of Partiality, in these Researches into a Subject of so delicate a Nature in itself, as the Intercourse between a Mother Country, and her Colonies; and more particularly so at this Time, and in this Instance.

In Order to give due Weight to what I shall say on this important Subject, it is necessary that I should explain the Origin and Extent of that Experience, which I hinted at in my first Letter, as the Reason that induced your Lordship to prescribe this Attempt to me.

I have

I have had the Honour to inform your Lordship of the Discoveries I made in the Year 1744; as also that since that Time I have traversed the whole Coast of *America, from Lat. 68 North,* to *Cape Florida;* and penetrated some thousands of Miles westward, into the Wilderness, many Parts of which, were never before trodden by European Foot.

The Accounts therefore, which I shall give of these, I had almost said boundless Regions, are not taken upon Trust, on the Relation of others. They are the Result of real Experience, on the Testimony of my Senses; as the Observations I shall offer on them are founded on the unerring Evidence of Facts.

The same Foundation of Experience also supports what I shall offer in Respect to the Commerce of the *West-Indian* Islands, as well as of the Colonies on the Continent.

In the Course of more than thirty Years, which I have been closely and constantly engaged in mercantile Business, in all its various Extent, I have had Intercourse in dealing with the Colonies of *Hudson's Bay, Newfoundland, Quebec, New England, Pensylvania, Virginia, North* and *South Carolina,* and *Georgia*------With *Barbadoes, Grenada, St. Vincents, Dominica, Antigua, Montserrat, Nevis, St. Christophers,* and *Jamaica*.------The Commerce therefore of these Places cannot reasonably be supposed to be unknown to me, or my Remarks upon it, only the chimerical Dreams of groundless Speculation, as has most shamefully been the Case with too many of those who have written on this important Subject.

A clear

A clear but concise Account of what particularly struck my Observation in the different Parts of *America*, with which I propose to begin, will be the best Introduction to those Hints of Improvement, which I would humbly suggest to your Lordship, in the Culture and Commerce of our Colonies there, and the most solid Basis, upon which to found the Expedience, and Practicability of them; and at the same Time afford the most convincing Proof of the inestimable Value of those Colonies to the Mother Country; and the indispensible Necessity in every Sense of political Prudence, of healing those unhappy Differences, which seem so alarmingly to threaten an Interruption at least, if not a total Loss of Intercourse with them, at this most critical Period.

It must not be expected though, that this Account shall include Descriptions of the Appearances of those Countries, or of the Persons, Manners, Customs, &c. of the Inhabitants. These Points have long been sufficiently set forth; or if any Curiosity concerning them still remains, it may soon and easily be gratified, by Recourse to the many Accounts extant of every Particular of this Kind in them. The Nature of the Soil, and its Aptitude by Climate and Situation for Agriculture and Commerce, in the Production of the Necessaries and Conveniencies of Life, both for the immediate Support and Use of the Inhabitants, and Communication and reciprocal Interchange with other Countries; and for the Transportation of them for such Interchange, and receiving the Returns of it, were the Objects of these Observations, which I here propose to submit to your Lordship's and the public Consideration; and from the Discussion of which, as I have said before, the Improvements that may be made in them, will naturally follow.

C

No more would I be understood to intend entering into the Disputes agitated at present between the Mother Country, and her Colonies, as a Partizan of either. I am too conscious of my own Insignificancy to obtrude my Sentiments on a Subject so much above my Sphere. Such Officiousness much oftener prejudices, than serves a Cause; the Pride of the human Heart turning away with Disdain from the Advice of an Inferior, however just and wise in itself, because the very Act of giving Advice implies a Superiority in that Instance.

I do not by this, my Lord, preclude myself absolutely from either of these Topicks, when in the Course of my present Undertaking, they shall fall naturally in my Way. Wherever the Manners and Customs of the present Inhabitants, Native or European, appear to me to influence the Interest of the Colony, either to its Advantage or Prejudice, I shall hold it my Duty to point out such Influence, and to suggest any Alteration of Manners or Customs, which I shall conceive likely to remove that Prejudice, or extend the Advantage.

The same Liberty I shall think myself entitled to, with Respect to the Systems of Policy adopted in the Administration of our Colonies both here, and on the Spot. Wherever they shall obviously appear to promote or clash with the Interests and Advantage of both in any Instance, *for seperated they cannot be*, I shall not hesitate to shew that Instance, and the Manner in which it is so affected, nor to suggest with proper Deference and Submission to better Information and superiour Power, what Means I think most efficacious to improve the former, and to remedy the latter.

I have the honour to be, &c. &c.

LETTER III.

MY LORD,

I SHALL begin this Review with one of the least noticed, but far from the least important in itself, of our Settlements, were the Advantages, obviously, and most easily to be made of it, properly attended to, which is that of *Hudson's-Bay*.

The Time, Manner, and Occasion of the Discovery of this vast Sea, and the Regions bordering on it, so far as they are yet discovered, are so well known, that it is unnecessary to recount them here.

Though the Design, which first led our daring Countrymen into the dark Recesses of the North, failed in its first Object, the Discovery of a Passage that Way to China, the Attempt failed not of producing other Consequences which well repaid to their Country, if not immediately to themselves, the Fatigue, Danger, and Expence of it to the bold Adventurers, by laying them under a Necessity of stopping, when the Severity of the Climate made the Seas no longer navigable, to explore their inhospitable Shores, for the Support of Life, 'till the Return of the Season proper for pursuing

suing their Project, whereby they opened with the Inhabitants an Intercourse of Commerce, unthought of before, and which but for this Cause, would never have been sought for through so many and such discouraging Difficulties.

The Seclusion of these Inhabitants from the more informed Part of Mankind by their Situation; and the Sterility of their Country, which confined their Cares within the narrow Circle of the indispensible Necessaries of Life, without supplying a single Article, that could suggest, much less gratify a Thought of any Thing farther, necessarily brought Commerce with them back to its original, of immediate Barter, or Exchange of one Commodity for another, without the Intervention of Money, the artificial Medium made use of in Countries of more extended Intercourse, and Produce, to supply the Defects, and remedy the Inconveniencies of such Barter.

The Advantages of such a Commerce to a Country able to avail itself of them are sufficiently obvious. It takes off such of its Produce and Manufactures as are most plenty, and cheap, at their real Value to those who want, and not being able to procure them elsewhere, beat not down their Price on Account of that Plenty, nor require such Accuracy and Ornament in the manufacturing of them, as make them come dearer to the Vender without being of greater Use to the Purchaser; and for any Deficiency in which they would be rejected by other Purchasers; and brings in Return the Produce of the Country of the Barterers, at the low Rate set upon it by those who do not want it, who have no other Vent for it, and consequently are glad to exchange it at any Rate for what

what they do want, and cannot obtain otherwife; not to dwell upon the great national Advantage of its being unmanufactured, and thereby affording Employment to the various Artificers, who prepare it for Ufe.

Thefe Circumftances were too ftriking not to be immediately perceived; but their Effect was circumfcribed in fuch a Manner by the very Means injudicioufly taken to improve and extend it, that what would have been a moft important Advantage to the whole Nation, was, by the Grant of *an exclufive Charter*, confined to a few Individuals, who actuated by the moft felfifh, fordid, and fhort-fighted Policy, or rather Cunning, reftrained, inftead of extending that Commerce, for Fear of its becoming an Object of publick Confideration, and the *Monopoly* of it taken from them, fhould the *(comparatively immenfe)* Profits which it might produce, be known; and thereby with the groffeft Difhonefty defeated intentionally, the exprefs End for which fuch Charter had been originally granted, on the moft plaufible Pretences, and ftrongeft Affurance to the contrary, and was ftill from Inattention, or Mifreprefentation, fuffered to remain with them.

This will be beft explained, and proved by the following Lift, and Eftimate of the feveral Articles exported from *England* to, and imported into *England* from this Settlement, which are drawn with the utmoft Exactnefs, and from the beft Authority.

COMMODITIES exported from ENGLAND to HUDSON's-BAY.

Coarse Woollen Cloths — Checks — Cottons — British Linens — Fowling-Pieces — Birding Guns — Gun-Flints — Gunpowder — Shot — Cutlasses — Wrought-Leather — Salt — Wheaten Meal — Oaten-Meal — Barley — Peas — Beans — Malt — Bacon — Beef — Pork — Butter — Cheese — Biscuit — Molasses — Wrought-Steel — Iron — Brass — Copper — Pewter — Pipes — Tobacco — Hosiery — Hats — Tallow-Candles — Ship-Chandlery — Stationary Wares — Bugles — Groceries — Oil — British Spirits — Wines — All which cost at an Average of three Years - - - } £ 16,000

The first View of these Lists, and Estimates will most probably be thought to contradict what has been advanced before of the Importance of this Settlement; but when it is considered that in the above List of *Exports* is included all that the Company sends for the Support and Maintenance of their Settlements, and for which consequently there can be no Return, as it is immediately consumed by their People —— When it is proved that the Commerce of it is kept thus low by Design, and the Means taken to accomplish that Design

COMMODITIES imported into ENGLAND from HUDSON's-BAY.

Thirty-four thousand Beaver Skins —— 16,000 Marten —— 2000 Otter —— 1100 Cat —— 3000 Fox —— 5000 Wolf —— 7000 Wolverine —— 650 black Bear —— 40 white Bear —— 500 Fisher —— 250 Mink —— 3000 Musquash —— 30cwt. to 50cwt. Bed-Feathers —— 20cwt. to 30cwt. Whale-bone —— A few Tons of Oil —— 150,000 Goose-quills —— 2000lb. Cut Beaver —— 1000 Elk —— 2000 Deer Skins —— 250lb. Castorcum —— Worth, as bought at the first Hand at QUEBEC, *at a like Average of three Years   -   -   -* } £ 29,340

Design are shewn, the Truth of my Position will appear in its full Force. But this must be the Subject of another Letter.

I have the Honour to be, &c.

P. S. Your Lordship will observe, that in estimating the *Imports* from *Hudson's Bay*, I strike the Price of them by that paid for the same Articles at *Quebec.*

The Reason of my doing this is, that the *Hudson's-Bay* Company conduct all their Affairs with such impenetrable Secrecy, that it is not possible to know at what Rate they exchange their Goods for those of the Natives; an Oath of Secrecy being imposed upon their Servants; and the Observation of all, upon whom they cannot impose such an Oath, prevented by the most brutal Inhospitality and Exclusion from every Kind of Intercourse.

Nor will *the gross Quantity of the Exports* open any satisfactory Insight into this Mystery; as it is not known, nor can, for the above Reasons be discovered with any Degree of Precision, how much of that Quantity is consumed by the Company's Servants; and consequently no Return for it brought Home in the *Imports*.

This much I know from my own Experience, that there is no fixed Rate for the Barter of any Commodity, the Company allowing just what they please, at that Time; in which Allowance, they are so equitable and reasonable, that I myself have seen Instances of their being conscientiously content with *a Profit of not above one thousand* per Cent. upon particular Articles.

These Lists therefore only shew what Advantage the Nation reaps at present, from the Commerce of this Settlement, under their *Monopoly*. What it would reap, were there no such *Monopoly*, with a more particular Account of the curious Methods taken to keep it in its present State of national Insignificancy, shall be shewn in the proper Place.

LET-

LETTER IV.

My Lord,

I HAVE shewn the present inconsiderable State of the Commerce to *Hudson's-Bay*. I have asserted that it is capable of such Improvement as would make it a considerable Advantage to the Nation. It remains now that I prove this Assertion. In doing this it will be necessary for me to look back for a Moment to Circumstances not attended to at present, but which have influenced this Commerce, from its very first Institution, and do still influence it, in the most pernicious Manner.

At the Time when the *Hudson's-Bay* Company was established, in 1670, the Minds of all People of Power, or Property, were so fixed upon the Intrigues of the Court, and the Consequences immediately apprehended from them at Home, that they would not spare a Thought for any Thing so remote in Situation and Effect, as *foreign Colonization*, by which Means that most important of political Enterprizes fell to those, who were in every Respect least qualified to pursue it to Advantage.

[18]

Under these inauspicious Circumstances, *an exclusive Charter* for trading to the Countries confining on the Sea, called *Hudson's-Bay*, was without enquiring into the Consequences, granted to a Set of private Adventurers, who without Support or even Countenance from Government, undertook upon the narrow Foundation of their own Fortunes to establish a Trade, attended with such Difficulties in Appearance, as would have discouraged any Men not fully perswaded of the Certainty of Success. Nor were they disappointed; the Event exceeding their most sanguine Expectations, in their very first Experiment.

Such Success from so weak a Beginning, shewed to an Height it might be carried, on a more extended Foundation. But the Scheme it suggested was very different: Instead of extending their first Plan, and making their Success known to procure an Enlargement of their Capital, the Company turned all their Care to conceal the whole, (which the Distractions of the Times gave them too good an Opportunity of doing) and keep the Profits of the Trade entirely to themselves, contracted as it was, rather than run the Hazard of their being shared in by others, should it be pushed to its natural Extent; a Care, which, as I have before observed to your Lordship, has never been relaxed since.

For this sordid Purpose, they contented themselves with proceeding on the low Capital, which Necessity had at first obliged them to set out upon, and making a few paultry Settlements, barely sufficient to carry on the restrained Trade which such a Capital could support. The Event has in this

also

[19]

alfo too well anfwered their Defign. The inconfiderable Amount of their *Exports*, and confequently of the *Returns*, have kept the Trade in fuch Obfcurity, as to feem beneath the Attention of Government, whereby it has remained, according to the Letter, however contrary to the Spirit of their Charter, *exclufively* in their own Hands.

It muft be owned that the Temptations to this Conduct were powerful. Without hazarding, or even advancing more than a comparative Trifle, they have long reaped, and do ftill reap a Profit, which a Capital ten Times as large could not produce in any other Channel of Commerce; a Reafon, which too many Inftances prove fufficient, in the prefent Times, to over-balance national Advantage, and juftify Breach of Faith; for by no other Name can fo manifeft a Violation of the Profeffions of promoting that Advantage, upon which all fuch Charters are granted, be called, without as manifeft a Violation of Truth.

I am aware, that it will be objected to this, by thofe who are interefted to keep thefe Affairs in their prefent State of Darknefs, that the *Imports* prove the Sufficiency of the Capital for the Trade, and that it is abfurd and unnatural to think any Men fhould be fo blind to their own Advantage, as not to make large *Exports* could they have adequate Returns for them. The latter of thefe Objections has been already obviated. I fhall now fhew the Fallacy of the former, and in what Manner the *Imports* are kept down to their prefent low Stand; low, I mean as to what they might be, for they are high beyond all parallel, confidering what they coft.

D 2 Though

Though the Natives of the vaſt Countries around *Hudſon's-Bay*, with whom the Traffick of the Company is carried on, are ſtill in that State of natural Ignorance, which People more informed, have arrogantly preſumed to call *ſavage*, Heaven has not denied them the Knowledge neceſſary for the few Purpoſes of their narrow Sphere of Life. They were not long engaged in this Traffick, therefore, before they diſcovered ſome of the groſs Impoſitions practiſed upon them, though they could not poſſibly form even a Conception of the whole.

I have obſerved to your Lordſhip, that the Commerce of the *Hudſon's-Bay* Company conſiſts in bartering ſome of our Manufactures and Commodities, the cheapeſt and worſt of their Kinds, with the Natives, for their Furs. The firſt Thing, which Reaſon would ſuggeſt to be done in ſuch a Traffick, by thoſe, who had the Lead in it, muſt be to fix the Rates of the ſeveral Articles to be brought by them for Barter, at ſuch a Standard, as ſhould obviate their being ever under a Neceſſity of altering it, and thereby raiſing a Suſpicion of Injuſtice in the others, who being neither able to judge of theſe Terms, nor of the accidental Circumſtances, which might at particular Times make an Alteration in them neceſſary, were they ſtruck with exactneſs, would certainly take Offence at ſuch Alteration, though they could not avoid ſubmitting to the firſt Eſtabliſhment, in the making of which I have not preſumed to mention the leaſt Regard to Juſtice.

But inſtead of this, a new Standard is arbitrarily impoſed by the Company every Seaſon, not on Pretence even of any
Alteration

Alteration in the Value of their own Commodities, or those of the Natives, but solely according to the Quantity of the latter, the whole of which be it more or less than on other Years, they calculate so as to get for their own, whose Quantity is nearly the same every Season. Such an Imposition was too glaring to escape unnoticed even by *Savages*, who though they could not shew their Resentment of it, in the same Manner, as People in other Circumstances, by discontinuing the Trade, yet did not fail to take the obvious Means of preventing it for the future, by bringing no more Furs, than their little Experience had taught them would suffice to procure in Exchange all the Commodities of the Company, the Quantity of which they also knew by Experience. The Remainder, for in their huntings for Food they slay many more of the various Animals, than they bring the Furs of to Market, they either consume themselves in Uses they might dispense with, could they turn them to any better Use, or actually throw away; practising out of Resentment the same Policy with the *Dutch*, in Regard to their superfluous Spices.

The Effects of a different Conduct must be the Subject of another Letter.

I have the Honour to be, &c.

My Lord,

THE Cause, and Consequences of the Conduct, which has been invariably pursued by the *Hudson's-Bay* Company, ever since it was established, having been considered, let us now consider what would be the Effect, had they adopted a different System, or rather had no such Establishment been made from the beginning, but the Trade left open in its natural State; indeed the only State in which any Trade can prove beneficial to a Nation, all *Monopolies* by their Principles counteracting the publick Interest, and setting up a private one in Opposition to it. The only Trade (or at least the only one worth taking any Notice of, carried on at present by the *Hudson's-Bay* Company, is the Fur-trade. But beside this, there are others already discovered, which if pushed to their proper Extent, would very soon not only equal, but most probably even exceed that; not to mention the Probability of discovering still more.

The first of these which I shall mention; and which to the Surprize of Reason has not hitherto been thought of any Consequence, is the Fishery. I will take upon me to say, that the Whale and Seal Fisheries in *Hudson's-Bay*, and *Baffin's-Bay*, are capable of affording sufficient, and sufficiently profitable Employment

ployment to several hundred fishing Vessels. Nor is this a vague Assertion. I speak it from Experience, having been some Years personally engaged in the Greenland Fishery, after my being at *Hudson's-Bay*, and gained a clear Insight into every Branch of it.

The Advantages which would necessarily result from this are most obvious. It would encrease the Numbers of our Seamen and Shipping, and every Branch of Commerce which does that, encreases the essential Strength of the Nation. And it would not only supply us with a Sufficiency of the Produce of these Fisheries for Home Consumption, but also give us the Command of the Trade so effectually, as to enable us to undersell all Rivals in it, at foreign Markets. That it is impossible for such a Trade to be carried on properly under the unnatural Restraints of an *exclusive Charter*, even were the Company to make the Attempt, is too evident to require Proof; and how much the Nation suffers by being secluded from it, may be judged from this one Circumstance, that instead of several hundreds of Vessels, and thousands of Seamen, which this single Trade would employ if laid open to publick Emulation, the whole Trade of the *Hudson's-Bay* Company employs no more than four Ships, and one hundred and thirty Seamen.

Another most valuable Article of Commerce, which those Countries would supply in the greatest Plenty, is *Copper*. In the Year 1744, I myself discovered there several large Lumps of the finest Virgin Copper, which in the honest Exultation of my Heart at so important a Discovery I directly shewed to the Company; but the thanks I met, may be easily judged from the

System

Syſtem of their Conduct. The Fact, without any Enquiry into the Reality of it, was treated as a chimerical Illuſion; and a Stop arbitrarily put to all farther Search into the Matter, by the abſolute Lords of the Soil.

The Advantages which would ariſe from a ſufficient Supply of this Metal, are alſo obvious to every Capacity. It would afford Employment to all our various Artificers who work in it; and enable us to underſell all Competitors at foreign Markets; and this at a Time, when our internal Supplies of it ſeem to be nearly exhauſted, and the Uſe of it is daily encreaſing in all Parts of the World.

I have ſaid, that Copper is to be found in Plenty in thoſe Countries, for this Reaſon. Wherever any Metal is found in Lumps, on or near the Surface of the Earth, it is a certain Proof that the Earth abounds with it deeper down; ſuch Lumps being protruded from the Body of the Metal, like Sparks from a large Fire. Nor is it unreaſonable to expect, that Metals ſtill more valuable might be found in the Purſuit of this; the richeſt Gold-mines in the Eaſt being intermixed with thoſe of Copper, as Copper itſelf is with Gold in Proportion to the Fineneſs of the former; and finer, than the Lumps I found there, have I never ſeen.

It muſt not be objected to what I have here advanced, that the Intenſity of the Froſt in thoſe Climates would defeat all Attempts of mining, or at the beſt render them ſo difficult and deſtructive to the Lives of the Miners, as to make it not worth the Attempt. This is only a vulgar Error.

Error. It is known that Frost penetrates but a little Way into the Earth; no farther than the immediate Action of the Atmosphere; where the Sphere of that Action therefore ceases, Frost ceases of Course; and the most ignorant Labourer knows that the deeper he can work into the Earth, the warmer Air he will breath.

I have the honour, &c.

LETTER VI.

My Lord,

HAVING traced the present State of the Trade to *Hudson's Bay* to its Cause, in the Conduct of the Company, and shewn some of the Consequences which would follow a different Conduct, the next Thing is to shew what that different Conduct should be.

The Impossibility of attaining to a just Knowledge of any Country, without first conciliating the Confidence of the Natives,

Natives, is clear to Reason, and has been proved by invariable Experience, as also that such Confidence is not to be conciliated, especially among *less informed* People, any Way but by long Acquaintance, much Intercourse, and many good Offices, to wear off the natural Shyness and Suspicion, inseperable from their being Actions not only new, but also incomprehensible to them.——In the Knowledge of a Country, I include its various Products, and Connections, as well as the exterior Face of it.

In order to this, the first Thing necessary (indeed indispensibly so) is to settle Colonies, to which the Natives may resort at all Times, to gratify Curiosity, carry on Commerce, or implore Assistance in any Circumstances of accidental Distress; and where they should always be received in an humane, and friendly Manner, without any Appearance of immediate Distrust, though at the same Time, without appearing to relax the Vigilance and Care necessary to preserve Respect, and obviate their being tempted by too great Security, to meditate any Thing hostile; which Colonies should be planted in as many different Parts of the Country, as consistent with Conveniency, to make the Acquaintance with the Natives as general as possible, and prevent the Misrepresentations, which are always made, by those who go between different People, for the Purposes of Trade, in order to enhaunce the Merit of such Mediation, and keep it exclusively to themselves; and this as well among *savage* as *civilized* Nations, from the same interested Views.

The

The Effects of such an Intimacy of Intercourse are most obvious. The hospitable Natives would communicate to their beneficent Guests, all the Knowledge which Nature had learned from Experience. They would shew them the Secrets of the Land, and assist them with their Labour to turn every Thing to their own Advantage.

These Reflections, my Lord, are applicable to the first Principles of Colonization. In the present Case, the Conduct here recommended, would have these particular good Effects. It would, in all human Probability, enlarge the Fur-Trade, the only Trade, as I have observed before, now carried on there, by the Discovery of Animals not sought after at present by the Natives, because their Flesh is not esteemed by them for Food, but whose Skins might be a valuable Addition to their Commerce; it would encrease the Consumption of our own Manufactures, in Proportion to the Increase of our Acquaintance with the Natives; and it would be the most certain Means of discovering that Passage to *India*, which first led our Mariners into those Seas, if any such Passage there is, or else put an End to the Trouble and Expence of making farther Attempts for such a Discovery; and so accomplish the first Object proposed by their Charter.

Nor are these the only Advantages which would result from the Establishment of such Colonies. They would necessarily extend to every other Branch of Commerce capable of being pursued here by habituating our People to the Climate and keeping them upon the Spot, by which Means they would be ready to commence their Work earlier, and able to pursue it longer in the Season, than they can at present, coming from afar, and obliged to get away soon, to save their Passage home.

The only Objections which can possibly be made to this, are the Want of People at Home to spare for planting Colonies; and the Improbability of their thriving in so severe a Climate. But upon the least Examination, both these Objections will vanish.

The Numbers of Beggars, who infest our Streets, shew that we have more People, than we can give Employment to, or at least, than will apply themselves to the Employments proper for them; and consequently, who can be well spared, to be sent elsewhere. It will be said perhaps, that while the Streets of our great Cities swarm, our Fields and Villages are thin; but this alters not the Case. Their Labour, not their Number is an Advantage to the Publick; and when that is discontinued, they become an Incumbrance to Industry, like Drones in a Hive, and had better even not to be at all, than to be supported at a Loss. 'Till it is thought proper therefore to put the Laws against such Vagrants, in Execution, or to frame others, if the present are insufficient to restrain the labouring People from leaving their own Settlements, where their Work is wanted, and crowding to the Cities, particularly the Metropolis, where there is not proper Work sufficient for them; every Scheme for removing them to Places, where they can get such Work, makes an Addition of that Work to the general Stock, and saves the Value of their present un-earned Consumption. Beside the Notion, that planting Colonies depopulates a Country has been long refuted, it being proved by Experience, that

in

in Countries where Induſtry is encouraged properly, there will always be as many Inhabitants, as there is good Room and Employment for, an encreaſed Generation, like Bees, ſupplying the Place of thoſe who go away; and it is the Want of this Induſtry, the Neceſſity of which is ſeemingly removed, by the Treaſures returned from her Colonies, that has depopulated *Spain*, not the Numbers of the People ſent to form thoſe Colonies.

As to the other Objection of the Climate, it is no more than a meer vulgar Error, derived from the ancient one of *uninhabitable Zones*, it having been long proved, that there is no Climate under Heaven to which the human Conſtitution cannot be reconciled by very little Care; the Neceſſity even of which Care would ceaſe with the firſt Settlers themſelves, as the Climate would be natural to their Children born and bred up in it.

Nor is there greater Weight in the Miſcarriage of the poor Attempts hitherto made to raiſe Corn, and Vegetables for the Support of theſe Colonies, in thoſe Parts of the Country which lie near to the Company's Forts; ſuch Miſcarriage being far from proving that better Succeſs might not attend more judicious Attempts made in other Parts, particularly on *Mouſe*, and *Albany* Rivers, which be nearly in the ſame Latitude with *London*. Or even ſhould all Attempts fail; Meal, Flour, Cheeſe, Butter, and eſculent Roots may be carried thither at an eaſy Rate, and Fiſh and Fleſh, particularly that of Fowls, are moſt excellent in their Kinds, and ſo plenty, as to be below Price.

Having thus, my Lord, ſhewn the Loſs ſuffered by the Nation, from the injudiciouſly granted, and more injudiciouſly

ously (not to give it an harder Name) conducted *Monopoly* of the Trade to *Hudson's-Bay*, and the natural and easy Means of preventing such Loss for the future, *on a Revocation of that Monopoly*, I must beg Leave to trespass upon your Lordship a little farther, while I lay before you a short View of the *present*, and *proposed* State of that Trade, brought together for Comparison.

The *Hudson's-Bay* Company employ four Ships, and 130 Seamen.———They have four Forts, which contain 186 Men.———And they export Commodities to the Value of £16,000 a Year, and bring Home Returns to the Value of £29340— which yield to the Revenue £3734.

If the Trade were laid open, the Fishery alone in *Hudson's-Bay*, *Baffin's-Bay*, and *Davis's Streights*, (in the last of which the *Dutch* find Fish as Plenty as in *Japan*, where they kill them solely for their Bone) would afford Employment for 800 Vessels of every Kind, and 16000 Men.———

The Trade would require and support Twelve Colonies, consisting of 3000 settled Inhabitants of both Sexes.—And, the Exports would in the Course of seven Years at the very farthest, amount to £320,000. the Returns to £586,800, which would yield to the Revenue £74,680, being twenty Fold the present Amount of each, with a certain Prospect of farther Increase. But so it is, that *all these national and great Advantages are sacrificed to fatten a few worthy Individuals.*—

I need not pursue the Subject any farther. The Inference, from what has been shewn, is obvious; and must open the

Eyes

Eyes of all, who are not determined to keep them shut. Happy for the Nation, that such is not your Lordship's Case! That you hold not yourself above receiving Information from your Inferiors; and that Heaven has blessed you with Ability to turn that Information to the best Advantage.

I have the Honour, &c.

P. S. Among the Things neglected by the *Hudson's-Bay* Company, and what will always be neglected by every *monopolizing* Company, as foreign to their immediate Profit, I have not made any Mention of civilizing the Natives, and instructing them in the Christian Religion, though to pass over the moral Duty of doing it, the great Advantages in Point of Interest, which the *French* have reaped from their Labours in this Way, in other Parts of the World, should be an Incitement to other Nations not to neglect it. ——

LETTER VII.

My Lord,

THE Country, I wish I could say Colony, that comes next under Consideration, in our Return from the No.th, is *Labrador*.

The strange Neglect of forming any Settlement in this Country, is one of those glaring Instances of the Blindness of Man to his best Interest, which prove the Insufficiency of his boasted Wisdom, and the indispensible Necessity of a ruling Providence to lead him right in the plainest Road. For though this Land does not immediately yield Gold, Silver, precious Stones, or those Foods for Luxury and Ostentation, which are in such mad Request, it would yield a Treasure much more solid, permanent, and advantageous to the Commonweal, in the Fruits of Industry, which encreases the Strength along with the Wealth of a Nation; Labour rewarded by Plenty invigorating the present Race, and encreasing Population, in its happiest Appearance, an healthy and vigorous Progeny.

The

The Climate on the Coast of *Labrador* is less severe, than that of the Countries confining on *Hudson's-Bay*. The Country is covered with Forests of valuable Timber, abounding with various Animals, whose Furs would be a most profitable Addition to our Trade in that Branch, and whose Flesh, in the general, is most wholesome, as that of the various Fowls with which the whole Country also abounds, is most delicious Food. The Soil, with proper Cultivation, is capable of producing Corn, and most Kinds of exculent Roots, and Vegetables; and the Rivers and Sea-Coasts yield Fish, excellent for Food, as well as Trade, in a Plenty, that almost exceeds Conception. All this is immediately on, or near the Sea-Coast; our Discoveries extending but a very little Way farther. Were the interior Parts of the Country known, it is more than probable, that many other Advantages would be discovered in them; and of this the Fewness of the Natives hitherto seen gives the strongest Presumption; it being much more agreeable both to Reason and Experience to suppose, that those few we see are only Vagrants, and that the Body of the People find Attachments to fix them in the Centre of their Country, than that such a Country should be so thinly peopled throughout.

The only Attempt hitherto made to carry on any Trade here, has been in the Fishery; which makes the following Exports yearly to *Great-Britain*, *Portugal*, *Spain*, and *Italy*.

Whale-Oil	–	1500 Tons	– at £15 –	£22,500	0 0
Seal-Oil	–	310 Tons	– at £15 –	4,650	0 0
Whale-bone	–	72 Tons	– at £300 –	21,600	0 0
Seal-Skins	–	12000	– at 6d. –	300	0 0
				£49,050	0 0

There are no Exports from *Great-Britain*, that can with any Propriety be placed against this. With the Natives we have no Trade. In the Country we have no Settlement; and the Consumption of the People, employed in carrying on the Fishery, is supplied by the different Places whence they come every Season, and whither they return at the End of it; and for the Time they stay, consists of the bare Necessaries of Life, and Implements of their Business, without entering at all into our Manufactures.

How different would the Case be were these Colonies established. The Advantages of such Establishments have been explained in the preceding Instance of *Hudson's-Bay*. All those enumerated there (except the local one relating to the *North-west Passage*) are applicable to this Country, in the strictest Sense. They would be filled with People of our own, whom it were a saving to the Publick to send abroad; or with People of other Nations, who allured with the Advantage, would settle with us, and become our own. They would turn to proper Advantage the Articles of Commerce already discovered there, and most probably discover still many more. They would take off our Manufactures, and send us in Return the Produce of the Country to be manufactured

factured by us; and they would necessarily encrease the Numbers of our Shipping, and Seamen, the best Wealth, and Strength of *Great-Britain*.

The Number of Colonies proper to be planted here, is not for me to determine. If we would begin with only two, or even one, the Experiment would soon prove its own Utility, and shew where, and in what Manner we should proceed farther.

I have the Honour, &c.

P. S. Another (and that a most important) Advantage that would arise from the Establishment of Colonies, on this Coast, is the convenient Opportunity it would afford of boiling down the Blubber, and making the Whale-bone merchantable on the Spot; by which Means they might be carried directly to Market, and the Loss of Time and Expence of bringing them Home in the Gross, as at present, saved.

LETTER VIII.

My Lord,

CONTINUING our Course from the North, we come next to the Island of *Newfoundland*. The Climate of this Island differs not very much from that of *Labrador*; and that Difference is still less to its Advantage, the heavy Fogs which hang over it, for so great a Part of the Year counter-ballancing any little Abatement in the Intensity of the Frost. The Country is well stock'd with Timber fit for the most valuable Purposes of Ship-building. It has many fine Rivers; and on the Coast are several large, commodious, and safe Harbours. But, on the other Hand, the Soil is so poor, and unfit for the Purposes of Vegetation, that the Heat of the Summer, though very great, cannot force it to produce any Thing in Plenty, or Perfection.

This is on, or very near the Sea-Coast, to which our Knowledge of the Country has been hitherto confined. When the interior Parts of it shall be known also, it is far from being in the least improbable, that this Complaint may

in

in a great Meafure ceafe, and many Advantages, as yet unthought of, be difcovered.

But it is not the Ifland, or its Produce, that is the Object of our Attention. It is the Cod-Fifhery on the Coaft, or as they are called, the Banks of *Newfoundland*, the greateft, and the beft Fifhery in the known World.

The Importance of this Fifhery to *Great-Britain* has been long and well known to the People of this Nation. Would to Heaven, it had been as well taken Care of by its Governors. At the Peace of *Utrecht* it was ceded to us by the *French*, and difcontinued by the *Spaniards*; but both foon broke through their Engagements, and refumed the Trade, not indeed avowedly in the Names of the refpective Nations; but in private, and feemingly clandeftine Attempts of Individuals, which were taken fo little Notice of here, if they were not even connived at, that the *French* in particular before the breaking out of the laft War, had gradually worked themfelves, into a great Share of it, which has been fince confirmed to them, at the Peace of *Paris*.

I muft not, my Lord, indulge my Thoughts upon this Subject! It is too late! The Deed is done, and all that remains now is, to remedy its Effects, as far as poffible; in order to do which, it is neceffary to take a diftinct View of the prefent State of this Trade.

COMMODITIES exported from *Great-Britain* and *Ireland*, to *Newfoundland*.

Coarse Cloathing — Cottons — Checks — British Linens — Guns — Gunpowder — Shot — Gun-Flints — Fishing-Tackle — Wrought-Leather — Wrought-Steel — Iron — Brass — Copper — Pewter — Pipes — Hosiery — Hats — Tallow-Candles — Ship-Chandlery — Stationary-Wares — Grocery — Oil — Bacon — Beef — Pork — Malt — British-Spirits and Wines —— All which at an Average of three Years cost - - - - - } £273,400

In carrying the above several Articles to *Newfoundland* from *London, Pool, Weymouth, Dartmouth, Tynemouth, Topsham, Bristol, Liverpool*, and different Parts of *Ireland*, and in bringing the Fish, and Oil to the several Markets in *Portugal, Spain*, and *Italy*; as also in catching and curing the said Fish, there are employed

Ships 380 - with Twelve Men in each
Boats 2000 - with Eight Men in each, } 20560 Men.
making together - - -

In the above List of the several Articles sent to *Newfoundland*, I have not included Salt — Wheaten-Meal — Oaten-Meal — Barley — Peas — Beans, &c. carried from *Philadelphia*, and our other *American* Colonies thither; which though they do not go immediately from *Great-Britain*, yet as they increase the Trade of those Colonies, their Profits consequently centre with her.

Exported from *Newfoundland*.

Cod-Fish	- 30,000 Tons	- at £ 10	- £	300,000
Oil	- 3000 Tons	- at £ 15	-	45,000

£ 345,000

The Ballance of £ 71,600 in the Favour of *Great-Britain*, which appears upon the Face of this State, is by no Means to be taken for the whole Amount of the Profits of the Trade. The Prices here set upon the Cod-fish and Oil, are only what they are worth upon the Spot. At the several Places where they are disposed of, they bring much more than twice that Sum; so that at the most moderate Computation, this Trade adds annually a clear Profit of more than half a Million to the Wealth of the Nation.

The Importance of such a Trade proves itself at the first View; and the Variety, as well as the Amount of the Articles exported, shews how extensively, and deeply it enters into our Manufactures; and the Numbers of the Seamen bred up in it, to every Hardship of that laborious Life, make it the Nursery of our Navy, and therefore one of the main Sinews of our most natural, most essential Strength.

Nor is this Importance bounded by its present State, prosperous as it is. The Prospect extends still farther; and I will be bold to say, that the Advantages reaped from this Fishery, may be doubled within the Course of a very few Years, if the proper Means are taken, and pursued with proper Vigilance, and Vigour.

I have

I have observed to your Lordship, that the Coast of this Island abounds with large, and safe Harbours. The first Thing to be done to improve the Trade to its natural Extent, would be to plant Settlements on such of these Harbours as lie most convenient to the Banks, for curing the Fish, where Stages, &c. should be erected of Strength sufficient for long continued Use, and preserved for it, so as to save the Expence, Inconvenience, and Loss of Time, experienced from the temporary ones now used.

As the Quantity of Fish upon the *Banks* is inexhaustible, by having such Settlements established, ready prepared for curing them, we should immediately be able to supply all our *West-India* Islands, with Fish for the Support of their Negroes, so much cheaper than the Way they are supported at present, that they would be able not only to supply the Mother Country with Sugars for Home Consumption, infinitely cheaper than at present; but also to undersell every other Rival in the Trade at foreign Markets.——

Let *Britain* ever preserve its hitherto unsullied Honour of keeping inviolable the Faith of Treaties!—— Let the *French* enjoy what they have gotten; but give them no more, nor let them encroach beyond the Bounds (too extensive already) indulged to them.

I have the Honour to be, &c.

LETTER IX.

My Lord,

WE will now, if your Lordſhip pleaſes, quit the Coaſt of the main Ocean, for a few Moments, and make a ſhort Excurſion up the great River *St. Lawrence*, to our newly-acquired Dominion of *Canada*.

The Advantages that muſt neceſſarily ariſe from this Country to *Great-Britain*, have been ſo lately, and ſo fully canvaſſed, as is the Caſe of all new Acquiſitions, that it cannot be neceſſary to enter into the Proof of them here. A bare Recital of a few of the moſt conſiderable for Reference, is all therefore which I ſhall treſpaſs upon your Lordſhip's Time with at the preſent.

By

By expelling an inveterate, active, and infidious Enemy from the Centre of our Colonies, on that vaſt Continent, we ſecure them from the Danger of being attacked from behind; and enable our People to attend with proper Spirit, and Induſtry, to the Improvement, and Extenſion of their Settlements in the interior, and more remote Parts of the Country, where the Fertility of the Soil, or any particular Production, or Convenience, may induce them to ſettle. It removes a rival Power out of the Sight of the Natives, and leaves them without Aſſiſtance, or even Hope of Impunity in any hoſtile Attempt againſt us. It brings their Reſource for all the Conveniencies of Life ſolely to ourſelves, and thereby puts us in the ſole Poſſeſſion of their Commerce. It gives us an Opportunity to puſh that Commerce to its full Extent, and to enlarge it with thoſe farther Diſcoveries of new Articles, which the little Experiments we have hitherto been able to make, give us juſt Reaſon to expect there. It affords Employment for a great Addition to the Numbers of our Ships and Seamen; and thereby encreaſes our national Strength.——And laſtly, it doubles all theſe Advantages ten-fold, in our Hands, by taking them out of the Hands of our Enemies.

Your Lordſhip will obſerve, that in ſumming up theſe Advantages, I ſuppoſe all proper Means to be taken for making the moſt of our Acquiſition. On the contrary Suppoſition, the whole will be reverſed. The Advantages will
ſlip

slip out of our Hands, and arm the Hands of our Enemies against us. Nor must this be looked upon as only meer Speculation, or raising Phantoms of improbable Danger. The Pertinacity, with which the *French* Crown insisted on the Restitution of the Island of *Cape-Breton*, when taken from them in the War before the last,—the enormous Sums expended in fortifying it for, and defending it in the last War,—and the Reluctance with which they gave up their Claim to it, after it had been again taken from, and was evidently impossible to be recovered by them, prove, beyond a Doubt, their Conviction of the Importance of this Country, for keeping in their own Hands the Command of the Navigation to which, as well as for the Support of their Encroachments upon us in the *Newfoundland* Fishery, these Fortifications were built, and defended; as our unvaried Experience of their political Faith, and Regard to Treaties sufficiently shews their Intention in the Infringements already made by them upon the Bounds set them by the Treaty of *Paris*; and must open our Eyes to what we are to expect, whenever they shall find a favourable Opportunity for setting up a Claim of Right to what they shall get hold of by such Infringments.

The best Means therefore of obviating such Intentions, are the proper Objects of our present Consideration; as the Efficacy of those Means will best appear from a Representation of the present State of our Commerce with that Country.

Commodities exported from *Great-Britain* to *Canada*.

Wollen-Cloths — British-Linens — Cottons — Checks — Callicoes, and sundry India Goods — Paisley Lawns — Guns — Cutlasses — Gunpowder — Shot — Gun-Flints — Haberdashery-Wares — Gold and Silver Lace — Wearing-Apparel — Cotton-Velvets — Stuffs — Hosiery — Hats — Gloves — Books — Stationary Wares — Drugs — Glass — Wrought-Leather — Wrought-Steel — Iron — Copper — Tin — Brass — Pewter — Pictures — Painter's Colours — Bees-Wax — Vermillion — Millenery Wares — Blankets — Sadlery Wares — Sail-Cloth — Cordage — Fishing-Tackle — Cheese — Tobacco-pipes — Strong Beer — British Spirits — Wines — All which cost at an Average of three Years - - - } £105,000

The above View of the Nature, and present Amount of this Trade proves beyond a Doubt the Practicability of pushing it to such an Extent, as must make it of the most essential Importance to this Nation. The Commodities it takes off are all, except the India-goods, immediately of our own Produce, and Manufacture; and the Returns it makes,

are

COMMODITIES imported from *Canada* into Great-Britain.

Ninety thousand Beaver Skins—9000 *Bear*—11,000 *Otter*—4000 *Fisher*—36,000 *Marten*—350 *Wolf*—4000 *Cat*—2000 *Mink*—2000 *Fox*—50,000 *Musquash*—100,000 *Racoon*—*Elk and Deer* 24,000—And 2000 *b*. of *Castorcum*	£ 76,000
Whale-bone—Whale, Porpus, and other Fish-Oil.	3,500
Wheat 12000 *Quarters at* 20s	12,000
Ginseng—Snake-root, and Capillaire—Sundry	3,000
Timber—Plank—Deals—Lumber, &c.	11,000
	105,500

Which Trade is carried on by 34 Sail of Ships, navigated by about 400 Men.

---

are in the *unmanufactured* Produce of that Country; which single Circumstance of their being unmanufactured, doubles their Value to us, by the Employment it affords to our Manufacturers, whose Labour is one of the chief Sources of our national Wealth. As to the Quantities both of those *Commodities*, and the *Returns* for them, the least Attention to the

Circumftances of the Country will fhew how fhort they fall of what they may be.

In all new Conquefts, the Inhabitants naturally have a Diffidence and Dread of their Conquerors, however humane in their Manner of waging war, and beneficial in their Meafures of governing after. If it fhould be objected in the prefent Inftance, that the only Inhabitants of this Country, who can properly be faid to have been conquered, are the *French*, the Natives only exchanging one Mafter for another, it alters not the Cafe. The Dominion, which the *French* had acquired over the Minds of the ignorant Natives, as well thofe apparently free and independent of them, as their immediate Subjects, by the Arts of their Priefts and Friars, always fuccefsful in Proportion to the Ignorance of thofe upon whom they are practifed; and the Animofity and Abhorrence which they inftilled into them againft us, have been feverely experienced in too many Inftances, during the whole Courfe of the War: While any of thefe Priefts and Friars therefore are permitted to remain among them to keep up thofe Prejudices, and fow the fame pious Seeds of Difcord and Hatred, it is in vain to expect, that the Natives fhould enter into fincere Amity, and Confidence with us.

The firft Thing therefore to be done, in Order to conciliate their Confidence, is to banifh effectually the *French Priefts*, and *Religious of all Denominations*, and to fend in their Room *a labouring Clergy of our own*, who breathing the true Spirit of Chriftianity themfelves, and practifing it in its moft facred Fruits of univerfal Benevolence, and Philanthropy, or in the

Phrafe

Phrase of holy Writ, in *Charity to all Men*, should set such an Example to their Flocks, as could not fail to eradicate their Prejudices against us, and implant in their Stead, Confidence, Respect, and brotherly Love.

The common Reproach brought even by ourselves against our Clergy, that they follow only the Loaves and Fishes of the Church; and are too lazy, and too much attached to the present Enjoyment of the good Things of this World, to labour in the Vineyard of their Lord; and bear the Heat and Burthen of the Day, in converting savage Nations to his Laws, must not be opposed to what I have here offered. The Pains taken to this End by some Individuals, in other Parts of *America*, and the Success with which Heaven has blessed those Pains, prove that our Religion gives not a Sanction to such Neglect of Duty; and that Protestants, can be as indefatigable in propagating the Gospel of Christ, as Papists of any Denomination whatsoever.

By *Protestants*, my Lord, I mean Christians *protesting* against spiritual Tyranny in all its Exertions, and obeying in the Freedom of Conscience the Laws and Doctrines of Christ, as explained by the best Power of Reason, without stooping to enter into the nominal Distinctions, into which the Restlessness of human Imagination, more than any real Difference, has divided that Name.

I must not, my Lord, be understood by thus urging the Banishment of the Popish Clergy to contradict myself, and propose a Practice opposite to the Principles of Christian Liberty

berty which I profess. Where the Principles of any Set of Men are professedly subversive of that Liberty, and expressly contrary to the most essential Principles of that Religion which they profess in common with us, the most, indeed the only effectual Way to preserve both, is to drive them out from among us; and that such are the Principles of those who assume to themselves a Right to put Shackles on the human Mind, and limit God's Mercies to the Profession of their own Opinions, is too evident to require Proof.

The *secular* Advantages to ourselves, which must necessarily follow from this Attention to the *spiritual* Welfare of these People are most obvious. Informed in their Minds, they would become civilized in their Manners. They would soften from that Ferocity, which prompts them to those barbarous Wars, and Murders, that have almost desolated their Country, and increasing in their Numbers would proportionably increase in their Demands for the Conveniencies of Life, with which our Trade supplies them; and would consequently apply themselves to procure an equivalent Encrease of their own Produce to give in Exchange for them. They would assist us with their Strength and Experience of their Country to improve the Trade at present carried on between them and us, and to prosecute with better Prospect of Success our Endeavours to enlarge it by the Discovery of new Articles. And by their Intercourse with us in the fraternal Amity of Religion, they would acquire Knowledge of the Excellence, and be glad to put themselves under the Protection of our Laws, and so in the End make their Numbers our Strength, and become one People with us.

In

In enumerating thefe Advantages, your Lordſhip may poſſibly be furprized at my confining myfelf to fuch as are immediately fecular. But in this I conform to the Humour (if I may fo call it) of the Times, to which Propofals for Practice muſt never run counter: But I live, my Lord, in Hopes of feeing better Times, when the Advantages of this Life fhall be held in Efteem only as they are conformable to the more valuable ones of that which is to come; and no Means purfued, at leaſt profeſſedly, to procure the former, which fhall not alfo conduce to the latter. And in this Hope I am, humanly fpeaking, confirmed by the Experience of all Ages, in which it has been invariably obferved, that when Things arrive at a certain Point, they always change; and if Immorality and Irreligion are not arrived at their Height among us, Lord have Mercy upon thofe who are to behold their Advance!—

The next, and only Thing farther, which I would propofe for the Improvement of this important Acquifition, is Agriculture. The other Branches of its Trade are in the Hands of the Natives, and fhould be left undifturbed with them, as beſt qualified to purfue them with Succefs, I mean the *Fur*, and *Peltry*-trades, for any Encreafe that can poſſibly be made in the former of which, either in this, or any other Part of our Dominions, or in any of the Countries where we have Settlements, we can never want advantageous Vent; and for a large Encreafe in the latter we have fufficient Room, and fufficient Reafon to expect that Encreafe, particularly in the Article of Deer-Skins, a much greater Quantity of which than is now imported could be brought with the greateſt Advantage into our Manufactures; but as for Tillage, they

H   do do neither underſtand, nor are yet ſufficiently ſettled in their Diſpoſitions to attempt it.

The *internal* Advantages of purſuing Agriculture, are ſufficiently known. It ſupplies Employment, and plenteous Support to the People, and that Plenty ſupplies more People to be ſupported and employed. Nor is this Article liable to be carried too far, as moſt others are, it being impoſſible that Bread ſhould ever be too plenty; the Mouths to eat it encreaſing in Proportion as there is Bread for them to eat; and *externally* it would enable us to ſupply with the Overflowings of our own Plenty, thoſe Countries which might ſtand in Need of ſuch Supplies; and this without Danger of ever interfering with the Corn-Trade of *Great-Britain*, or our other Colonies, there being, as I have before obſerved, a ſufficient Demand for both, and that neareſt hand being always the firſt taken off.

The Quantity of Corn at preſent exported from *Canada*, has been ſhewn to be 12000 Quarters; but this is rather a Proof that the Country can produce Corn, than any Meaſure of its Production; as I will be bold to ſay, that fifty Times that Quantity may be produced annually without neglecting proper Attention to any other Branch of Commerce.

In a Word, my Lord, by proper Application to this ſingle Article of Agriculture, *Canada* may be made within the Compaſs of a few Years, to reimburſe to *Great-Britain*, all the Blood and Treaſure, expended in the Conqueſt of it.

I have the Honour, &c.

LETTER X.

My Lord,

FROM *Canada*, we will defcend with the Stream to *Nova Scotia*, a former Acquifition from the fame Power, fituate on the Mouth of the River *St. Lawrence*.

Though this Province has been in our Poffeffion above half a Century, fince the Peace of *Utrecht*, little or no Advances were made in the Settlement of it, 'till after the War before the laft, when a moft numerous Colony, amply provided with every Thing neceffary, was fent and fettled there, and an excellent Dock-yard, &c. built for the Service of the Navy, ftationed in thofe Parts of *America*, with good Houfes for the Officers and Artificers employed in it, and Barracks for the Army, compofing together the handfome Town of *Hallifax*, all at the great Expence of Government. But the Succefs has no Way anfwered this Expence, except fo far as it refpects the particular Service of the Navy; the only Advances made in cultivating and improving the Country, being confined within the narrow Limits of the immediate Environs of the Town, all at any Diftance remaining in the fame unprofitable State as before; fo that there is not a fufficient Supply of the poor Products of the Place even for the Inhabitants, who instead of being able to make any Exports, are obliged to depend for their own Support upon our other Colonies; which they would not be able to pay for, but for the Money spent among them by the Navy, and the Army; the only Benefit received by them from the latter, who are found totally incapable of defending them from the Outrages of the Natives. How far this Benefit may be equivalent to the Expence; and whether Part of that Expence might not answer the End better, if applied in another Manner, not to mention the Loss of so many Men's Labour and Lives, the Scurvy carrying them off in Numbers, are Points well deserving the Attention of Government.

As to the Navy, the Advantage to that is very great, as the Shipping have not only a safe and convenient Harbour to be laid up in, during the Winter Season, when all Navigation is impracticable in those Seas; but can also be repaired, and supplied with any Thing they may want, without the Fatigue, Danger, and Loss of Time of coming Home, upon every Occasion of the Kind, as heretofore.

The Miscarriage in the Settlement of this Province, must not be attributed solely to any insuperable Incapacity in the Province itself. The Climate, though far from being the best, or most agreeable, is yet equally far from being unwholesome, or unfit for the Purposes of Vegetation, if taken timely Advantage of, nor is the Soil so poor, but that with proper Cultivation and Care, it would produce the most valuable of all vegetable Productions, Wheat in great Plenty; and many of the esculent Plants and

Roots

Roots in Requeſt among us, if not in ſo high Perfection as other Countries, yet wholeſome and good for Uſe.

The true Reaſon of this Miſcarriage, is the inveterate Hoſtility of the Natives, who, though very few in Number, yet by lying in wait always, and in all Places, frequently find Opportunities of committing the moſt horrid Cruelties and Murders upon the Settlers; and even where they fail of this, they keep them in ſuch a State of continual Alarm and Dread, that they cannot apply themſelves to make any laſting or conſiderable Improvement.

An Enquiry into the Cauſe of this Malignity in the Natives towards our People is not ſo immediately to the preſent Purpoſe. The firſt Thing neceſſary to be done is to guard againſt the Effects of it; and for this, ſad Experience has proved that *European* Soldiers are utterly unqualified, being neither active enough in themſelves, ſufficiently acquainted with the Country, nor ſufficiently inured to the Severity of the Climate, to watch and purſue an Enemy poſſeſſed of all theſe Advantages, and actuated by the keeneſt Hatred and Animoſity. Inſtead therefore of ſending Soldiers from hence, the moſt effectual Means to put an End to the Inroads of theſe Savages, obviouſly is to procure a Body of the Natives of ſome of the neighbouring Colonies, moſt firmly attached to us to encounter them. Theſe, from the natural Ferocity of their Diſpoſition, might be brought at a very trifling Expence, comparatively to what we are now at to no Purpoſe; and when once let looſe upon the others, would in a very ſhort Time eſtabliſh the Country in a State of Safety, by cutting off all

thoſe

those actually engaged in Hostilities, and whom Experience has proved it to be impossible to reconcile to us; and taking the rest of all Ages and Sexes Prisoners, to be dispersed among other distant Colonies, where they should not imbibe, nor have an Opportunity of practising such Prejudices.

I am very far myself, my Lord, from approving of the Extirpation of the Natives of any Country, by their Conquerors; and even if I did, have the Honour of knowing your Lordship too well to venture such a Proposal to you. But here the Case is very different. The Country is so large, and so very thinly inhabited, that our Settlements upon it can hardly be called an Intrusion, and are by no Means even an Inconvenience to the Inhabitants; notwithstanding which, and notwithstanding all the Advantages held out by us to them, we have ever found it impossible to subdue their savage Hatred in the least; so that this Severity against them is sanctified by the great, and eternal Law of Self-preservation. The Safety of the Settlers being once established, they would be able to seek out, and establish their Settlements in the Places, most fertile in themselves, and most convenient for their different Purposes of living and Commerce; and soon make such Returns, particularly in Wheat, Hemp, and Flax, for the Production of which, the Soil of the Country is in most Places excellently adapted, as would amply reimburse the Expence of sending them thither.

Our

Our Exports to *Nova Scotia* at present consist of the following Articles.

Woollen-Cloths—Foreign and British Linens—Wrought-Iron—Steel—Brass—Pewter—Tin—Hats—Hosiery—Haberdashery—Millenery, and Turnery-Wares—Sail-Cloth—Cordage—Ship-Chandlery-Wares—Fishing Tackle—Sadlery-Wares—Gold and Silver Lace—British Spirits—Wines, and Medicinal Drugs, which cost at an Average of three Years — — — } £ 26,500

The Articles exported from *Nova Scotia*, are

Salted Mackarel and Shads, 3000 Barrels at 20s. —	£ 3000
Cod-Fish 2500 Tons at £10 — —	25,000
Fish-Oil, 300 Tons at £15 — —	4500
Whale-bone, 5 Tons at £300 — —	1500
Ship, and other Timber, Masts, Lumber, &c. —	4000
	£ 38,000

By this State, the Trade of this Country appears to consist entirely of Timber, and the Produce of the Fishery; but if if it were once well settled, not only these might be advanced (the latter to more than double its present Amount, and the former without Bounds, as the Forests cover the whole Face of the Country) but also a new and most advantageous Trade be opened in the several Articles of Tillage before enumerated; beside what more might be struck out, upon Experience, and a better Knowledge of the interior Parts of the Country.

I have the Honour, &c.

LETTER XI.

My Lord,

WE will now take a Trip, for a few Moments from the Continent to the adjacent Islands of *St. John's*, and *Cape-Breton*.

The Island of *St. John's* differs very little in Climate, but most materially in Soil, from *Nova Scotia*; the latter being much fitter for Tillage, and the former for Pasture. But this Difference

Difference is far from a Disadvantage to either, as it gives Rise to an Interchange of their respective Products, in its Nature necessarily attended with Advantage, which their Nearness to each other frees from all Inconvenience, or Danger of Interruption.

While the Inhabitants therefore of *Nova Scotia* apply themselves to Agriculture, those of *St. John's* may turn their Lands to Pasturage; and thereby not only have their Time more at Command to pursue their own Fishery; but also be able to supply those engaged in the other Fisheries with Beef for their Support, and to establish a most profitable Trade in that Article, with the *West-Indian* Islands, where it will always meet abundant Vent.—I do not mean by this, that *Nova Scotia* is utterly unfit for Pasturage; or *St. John's* for Agriculture. I only speak of the Produce, for which each is most fit, and which consequently it must be their Interest to pursue principally, as a Point of Commerce.

The Spirit, with which the Settlement of this Island was undertaken immediately at the Conclusion of the last War, and the Numbers, Rank, and Wealth of the Persons engaged, gave Reason to expect a farther Progress by this Time, than appears to have been yet made in it; but whatever has been the Cause of the Delay, it is to be hoped that the bad Consequences of it are sufficiently seen; and that the Undertaking will be re-assumed with Effect.

As to the Island of *Cape-Breton*, its Importance consists solely in its Situation, of which the *French* took sufficient Advantage,

Advantage, while it was in their Poſſeſſion, for the Protection of their own and Annoyance of our Fiſhery upon the Banks of *Newfoundland*. But that Importance has ceaſed upon its falling into our Hands, who are in the acknowledged Superiority of Poſſeſſion of the whole Fiſhery; and therefore the Fortifications erected by them for their Purpoſes, have been demoliſhed by us, as not being of Uſe equivalent to the Expence of maintaining them.

The Iſland though does not thereby loſe all Uſe to us; for as the Cod-Banks extend up to, and all along the Coaſt of it, it affords a convenient Station for curing the Fiſh caught there, without the Trouble, Delay, and Expence of carrying them to any other Place for that Purpoſe; not to dwell upon the Importance of its Harbour, to the Navigation of the River *St. Lawrance*.

Other Purpoſes it can anſwer but very few; the Climate being ſtill worſe than that of *Nova Scotia*, and the Soil more unfit for Vegetation of every Kind, both on Account of the Rockineſs of the Iſland itſelf, and its Expoſure equally to the Cold of Winter, and Heat of Summer, there being no Foreſts to ſhelter Cultivation from them, as on the Continent. To attempt making any permanent Settlements therefore on this Iſland, muſt be in vain, as they can never ſucceed ſufficiently to induce the People to ſtay, or to reimburſe the Expence.

I have the Honour, &c.

LETTER XII.

My Lord,

I AM now come to *New England*, a Country that well deserves that Name, as being both the first, and greatest Colony established by us in *America*.

The Climate, Soil, and Produce of this Country are so well known, that any Account of them here must be utterly unnecessary: It's Importance to the Mother Country will sufficiently appear in the following State of the Trade carried on between them.

Commodities exported from *Great-Britain* to *New England.*

Wrought-Iron, Steel, Copper, Brass, Pewter and Lead—Wollen-Cloths—Stuffs—Flannels—Colchester-Bays—Long-Ells—British, Irish, and Foreign-Linens—Silks—Gold and Silver Lace—Millenery, Haberdashery, and Hosiery-Wares—Hats—Gloves—Manchester Goods—Birmingham and Sheffield Wares--Hemp—Sail-Cloth—Cordage Upholstery, and Sadlery Wares—Cabinet-Maker's Goods—Painter's Colours—Ship-Chandlery Wares—Earthen Ware—India Goods—Grindstones—Fishing-Tackle—Cheese—Pickles—Toys—Seeds—Tobacco-pipes—Strong Beer—Wines—Spirits—Medicinal Drugs—All which cost at an Average of three Years. - - - - - - } £395,000

The above Amount speaks for itself; but when the Nature of the Trade is considered, and that most of the Articles exported from *New England* being carried to other Markets, the greatest Part of the Returns made to us for our

Commodities imported from *New England*.

Cod-Fish dried — 10000 Tons - at £ 10 - £	100,000
Masts, Boards, Staves, Shingles, and Joists -	45,000
Ships about 70 Sail — — at £ 700 -	49,000
Pickled Mackarel and Shads, 8000 Barrels at 20 s -	8,000
Whale and Cod-Oil, 7000 Tons - at £ 15 -	105,000
Whale-bone — 28 Tons - at £ 300 -	8,400
Turpentine, Tar, and Pitch 1500 Barrels at 8 s -	600
Horses and live Stock — — — —	12,000
Potash — 8000 Barrels — at 50 s -	20,000
Pickled Beef and Pork - 9000 Barrels at 30 s -	13,500
Bees-Wax, and sundry other Articles, valued at an Average of three Years - - -	9,000
	£ 370,500

our Exports are in the Money for which their's are sold, the Consequence of it will appear in a still stronger Light.

It is most delicate, my Lord, to mention any thing that may seem to allude in the remotest Sense to the unhappy Disputes
at

at present subsisting between *Great-Britain* and her *American* Children. I shall therefore only observe, that if the Trade of this Colony, on it's present Footing, is so advantageous, what must it have been before those Disputes arose, when our Exports thither amounted to near £ 550,000 per Annum? And what should we not do to bring it back to that Amount?

The Complaints made by the Colonies (this along with the rest) of the Scarcity of Coin among them, must not be taken to invalidate what I have here advanced of our being paid in Money, for the greatest Part of our Exports to *New England*. The Fact is the very Reverse. That Money comes not immediately from thence, but from the Countries where her Commodities are vended, whence it is brought directly to us, the Imports of *New England* from all other Countries but *Great-Britain*, being too inconsiderable, to have any Weight in the Scale of Commerce; so that the Scarcity of Coin there proceeds necessarily from their paying us in Money, instead of preventing it.

If it should be enquired how this Colony can dispense with the want of the several Articles of Commerce, their discontinuing to take which, as formerly, has made such a Fall in our Exports thither, the Answer is obvious. It appears from the foregoing State of these Exports, that by very much the greatest Part of them consists of the Luxuries, or at best the *dispensible* Conveniencies of Life, the Country supplying the Necessaries in abundance. Now, as the Inhabitants pride themselves more than any other People upon Earth in that

Spirit

Spirit of Freedom, which firſt made their Anceſtors leave their native Country and ſettle there; and do really, as Individuals, enjoy more Independency, from ſeveral peculiar Circumſtances in their Manners, Laws, and Situation, it is natural to conceive that upon the firſt Apprehenſion (whether juſtly founded or not makes no difference!) of any Invaſion of that Freedom, and Independency, they ſhould take Fire, and ſacrifice to Reſentment, (May I not ſay virtuous Principle?) the Paſſions whoſe Gratification conſumed thoſe Articles of Convenience and Luxury, and confine themſelves to meer Neceſſaries. That they have already begun to do this, is too well known and felt. How much farther they may proceed in it, is far from being pleaſing in the Proſpect. Such Principles gain Strength by Practice; and that Practice will ſoon make thoſe Wants, which at the firſt may have been moſt painful, become ſo familiar as to be no longer felt.

I am well aware, my Lord, that this contradicts the Notion of a *neceſſary* Dependence upon us for thoſe Articles, which by artful and induſtrious Propagation has become popular here. But upon a proper Enquiry, this Notion will be found unable to ſupport itſelf. The People of *New England* owe that Independency of Individuals, in which the very Eſſence of true Liberty exiſts, and which is the beſt Protection of it, to a particular Law of Inheritance, by which the Poſſeſſions of the Father are divided equally among all his Children; ſo that they are kept in that happy Mediocrity, which by obliging them to turn their Thoughts to Induſtry, in order to avoid Want, exempts them from Temptation to,

as

as well as denies them the Means of gratifying Luxury; and at the same Time, by supplying them with a Foundation for that Industry to work upon, exempts them also from the Necessity of submitting to any Encroachment on their Liberty. A State, which they are known not to be yet refined enough in their Taste, to hazard, much less barter, for any Gratification whatsoever; and consequently the *Necessity* of their Dependence for such Gratification, is meerly imaginary.

I have before observed to your Lordship, that the Products of which this Country is capable, are sufficiently understood. The only Articles in which there is Room for Improvement are Hemp and Flax; Commodities for the Production of which their Soil and Climate are peculiarly proper, and of which it is impossible for us to raise too much, even for our own Consumption.

The Advantages which must *necessarily* arise from our having a sufficient Supply of these most essential Articles offer themselves to View, at the first Mention of it; nor can the Interest of any Set of Individuals engaged in that Channel of Trade by which they are at present supplied, deserve to be put, but for a single Moment, in Competition with that of the Nation in General, so nearly concerned in having this Trade brought home thus to ourselves.

I have the Honour, &c.

LET-

LETTER XIII.

My Lord,

THE Colonies of *Connecticut*, *Rhode Island*, and *New Hampshire* come naturally under Confideration next after *New England*, of which they originally were, and ftill in moft Refpects may be confidered as a Part; the Obfervations therefore made upon that are all neceffarily applicable to thefe it's younger Brethren.

The Produce of thefe Colonies is moftly the fame as that of *New England*; and their Trade with *Great Britain* carried on in the fame Articles, and fo blended with it, that it is more difficult, than it may feem neceffary, to draw the Line between them in many particulars. However, in order to throw as much Light as poffible upon fo interefting a Subject, I here lay before your Lordfhip a State of their feperate Trade, as far as it is carried on with any apparent Separation.

Commodities exported from *Great-Britain* to *Connecticut*, *Rhode-Island* and *New Hampshire*.

Wrought-Iron, Steel, Copper, Brass, Pewter and Lead—Wollen-Cloths—Stuffs—Flannels—Colchester-Bays—Long-Ells—British, Irish, and Foreign-Linens—Silks—Gold and Silver Lace—Millenery, Haberdashery, and Hosiery-Wares—Hats—Gloves—Manchester Goods—Birmingham and Sheffield Wares—Hemp—Sail-Cloth—Cordage Upholstery, and Sadlery Wares—Cabinet-Maker's Goods—Painter's Colours—Ship-Chandlery Wares—Earthen Ware—India Goods—Grindstones—Fishing-Tackle—Cheese—Pickles—Toys—Seeds—Tobacco-pipes—Strong Beer—Wines—Spirits—Medicinal Drugs—All which cost at an Average of three Years - - - - - - - } £ 12,000

The Difference between these Exports, and those of *New-England* is evidently no other than is always, and every where between different Parts of the same Country, all the Articles in the above List being included in that of the Exports of *New England*, as Part of an Whole.

As

COMMODITIES exported from *Connecticut, Rhode-Island* and *New Hampshire.*

Masts, Boards, Joists, Staves, &c. - -	£ 30,000
*Salted Beef—Pork—Hams—Butter—Cheese—Callivances—*and *Flax Seed* - - -	15,000
Whale and other Fish-Oil, 1500 Tons - at £ 15 -	22,500
Pickled Mackarel, Shads, and other Fish - - -	7,000
Horses and live Stock — — — —	25,000
Potash — 6000 *Barrels* — at 50 s -	15,000
	£ 114,500

As to the Balance against *Great Britain,* upon the Face of this State, it is only in Appearance. Their Trade directly with us has been shewn to consist almost totally in the Conveniencies nearest to being absolutely necessary to Life. If therefore it may appear that they do not take from us a Quantity of these, proportioned to their Numbers, the Reafon is, that they get them nearer at hand from the other Colonies, particularly *New York*, and *New England*, who in a great Measure carry on their Trade for them; so that the Produce of the Excess of their Exports over their Imports is to be placed to the Credit of those Colonies, and centers ultimately with us, as I have had the Honour to intimate to your Lordship in the preceeding Letter.

And now, my Lord, as the four Colonies of *New England*, *Connecticut*, *Rhode Island*, and *New Hampshire* are so inseperably connected with each other in every Sense, I shall here lay before your Lordship some farther Hints concerning them, which will probably be found to affect the general Interest of them all; and consequently that of *Great Britain*, which is as inseperably connected with them.

As the Importance of the Colonies arises solely from the Numbers of their Inhabitants, not from any Production of their own, or Advantages of Situation for Commerce peculiar to them; the first Thing to be thought of, is how to turn those Inhabitants to such Pursuits, as shall best supply their Necessities, and at the same Time engage their Attention too closely to give them Leisure for forming those Schemes, which Contemplation of their Numbers might, in a State of Idleness, suggest to them.

For this Purpose the two Objects evidently most proper (if not solely so) are Agriculture and Manufactures; but these are to be proposed to their Pursuit, on very different Principles.

Agri-

Agriculture, as hath been hinted before, is impoſſible to be puſhed too far, Conſumers encreaſing regularly with the Encreaſe of the Subject to be conſumed; and a Foreign Demand being always certain for any Exceſs of Home Conſumption. But in reſpect to Manufactures, a very different Conduct is to be obſerved. Inſtead of giving a general and indiſcriminate Encouragement to every Exertion of Art, as in *Great Britain*, their Endeavours ſhould be delicately and judiciouſly directed to ſuch particular Objects, as there may be juſt Reaſon to expect their ſucceeding in; and theſe are the immediate Neceſſaries, or at leaſt the almoſt indiſpenſible Conveniencies of Life.

I muſt not, my Lord, be underſtood to inſinuate, by this, a natural Incapacity in the Inhabitants of theſe Colonies for any Arts. The Contrary is well known. All I intend by this Limitation is, that their Capacities ſhould be applied to ſuch Arts as the Materials and Circumſtances of their Country are proper for bringing to Perfection; and as are exerted in producing thoſe Manufactures, which the poorer Part of the People are not able to purchaſe, and cannot, or at leaſt will not diſpenſe with the want of, without Diſcontent.

I am well aware, that ſelfiſh, ſhort-ſighted Politicians will inſtantly take the Alarm at this; and exclaim that what I propoſe for the Benefit of theſe Colonies muſt neceſſarily be an equal Prejudice to the Mother-Country. But I hope to prove, that the Contrary is the Fact; and that the moſt effectual Way of making them ſerviceable to us, and that in the moſt extenſive and important Senſe, is by encouraging them firſt to ſerve themſelves, by purſuing theſe two Objects.

The sound and salutary Policy of promoting Agriculture is too well, and too univerfally known to require Proof. The firſt and greateſt Advantages ariſing from it, are it's ſupplying Employment and Suſtenance at the ſame Time. In the preſent Inſtance the Application propoſed to Manufactures effects the firſt, and comes neareſt to the ſecond of theſe Advantages, there being many Manufactures, ſcarcely, if at all, leſs neceſſary to Life, than Bread itſelf. Where theſe therefore cannot be fabricated immediately by the Conſumers themſelves, their Eyes are neceſſarily turned to thoſe Places, where they may be purchaſed; and if they want Money, the common Medium of ſuch Purchaſe, that Want is ſupplied by Barter of the Things in their Poſſeſſion.

Thus far it may appear that the Progreſs is on right Principles; and ſo in the general it is. But particular Circumſtances make a material Difference in the preſent Caſe.

It has been ſaid that the Importance of theſe Colonies conſiſts ſolely in the Numbers of the Inhabitants; and that theſe Inhabitants enjoy a State of Independence in a Manner peculiar to themſelves. But it muſt be obſerved alſo that the very Means by which that Independence is preſerved to them, by keeping them at the ſame Time in a State of Poverty prevents their conſuming a Quantity of the Manufactures of the Mother-Country proportioned to their Numbers, and even confines their preſent ſcanty Conſumption to thoſe Articles on which the Profit of the Manufacturer is the loweſt.

To free them therefore from this Poverty, without undermining

mining their Independence, is the readiest and most effectual Method of turning their natural Importance to our Advantage; and this can be done easiest, if not indeed only, by the Encouragement here proposed to be given to Agriculture and Manufactures; the former, by supplying them with Sustenance, and a Stock to trade upon, which will never fail of a Market; and the latter by enabling them to make a sufficient Quantity of those other Necessaries, for which they now barter that Stock, and thereby leaving it in their Hands, to barter for other Conveniencies of greater Price, which they cannot reach in their present Circumstances, though they repine for, and never will be content without them.

Let the Inhabitants of these Colonies, I say, be properly encouraged to raise Flax and Hemp, to tan the Hides of their Cattle, to spin the Wool of their Sheep, &c. &c. &c. and work them up into the most immediate Necessaries; and they will then be able to apply the Price of their Exports, which now goes to purchase those Necessaries, to the Purchase of other Articles, less necessary, but of greater Price and Profit to the Vender; and not only this, but they will also exert their Industry to provide still more for Exportation, as soon as they become acquainted with the Enjoyments thus procured for them.

Nor is this the only Advantage that will arise from this Measure. It will divert them from the *carrying* Trade, the only Track in which they can possibly interfere with us, and leave it entirely in our Possession, by turning their Thoughts wholely to internal Pursuits; an Advantage, so obvious, and great that the very Mention is sufficient to enforce every Means for obtaining it.

It

It must not be objected, that the Increase of Population, which would necessarily follow such an Application to Agriculture as is here proposed, might be an Incouragement to attempt shaking off Dependence upon *Great-Britain*. That is only the Fear of a most contracted Policy. Our Possessions on that Continent exceed any Uses to which the Power of Imagination can assign them. While the Inhabitants therefore find Room for extending their Settlements interiourly, and a certain Vent, and satisfactory Return for the Produce of them, they will never think of breaking the Connection, from which they experience such Advantage; and by the Breach of which they cannot expect even to keep, much less to improve that Advantage. And this is that Commercial Dependance, which has been so much talked of, and so little understood of late: A Connection which, cemented thus by mutual Advantage would become indissoluble, and make their Numbers our Strength, as I have observed in another Instance.

These, my Lord, are some of the Hints, I proposed submitting to your Lordship's Attention, under which I flatter myself that they may be improved to the End for which they are humbly offered. Others, not less important, are reserved for another Place, as being more general in their Nature, and equally applicable to others of our Colonies.

I have the Honour, &c.

LETTER XIV.

My Lord,

THE next Province, that in Course offers itself to your Lordship's Consideration, is *New York*, in every Respect the happiest for Habitation in all *North America*; the Healthfulness of the Climate vying with the Fertility of the Soil; which not only produces aboriginally every Necessary of Life, but also brings all the vegetable Productions of *Europe*, that have been tried there, to Perfection, and many of them in a much higher Degree, with little or no Trouble, than they arrive at in *England*, under the most careful and expensive Cultivation.

Our Acquaintance with this Country is in every Sense so intimate, that it must be unnecessary to enter into any particular Account of it here: I shall therefore only lay before your Lordship the following View of the Trade at present carried on between it, and *Great-Britain*, as the most proper Introduction to the few Remarks which I shall beg Leave to hint to you thereupon.

COMMODITIES exported from *Great-Britain* to *New York.*

*Wrought-Iron, Steel, Copper, Pewter, Lead, and Brass—Cordage—Hemp—Sail-Cloth—Ship-Chandlery—Painter's-Colours— Millinery—Hosiery— Haberdashery— Gloves— Hatts— Broad-Cloths—Stuffs—Flannels—Colchester Bays—Long Ells—Silks—Gold and Silver Lace—Manchester Goods— British, Foreign, and Irish Linens—Earthen-Wares—Grindstones—Birmingham, and Sheffield Wares—Toys—Sadlery—Cabinet-Wares—Seeds—Cheese—Strong-Beer—Smoking-Pipes—Snuffs—Wines—Spirits—Drugs—*All which cost at an Average of three Years - - -   } £531,000

The high Amount of our Exports plainly shews the Importance of this Trade to the Mother-Country; but this Importance will appear in a still stronger Light, when it is considered that the greatest Part of the Exports of this Province are carried to other Markets, and consequently the Returns for

COMMODITIES exported from *New York* to *Great-Britain*, and other Markets.

Flour, and Biscuit, 250,000 Barrels at 20 s — £	250,000
Wheat, 70,000 Quarters at 20 s — —	70,000
Beans, Peas, Oats, Indian Corn, and other Grain -	40,000
Salt-Beef, Pork, Hams, Bacon, and Venison —	18,000
Bees-Wax 30,000 lb at 1 s — —	1,500
Tongues, Butter, and Cheese — —	8,000
Deer, and other Skins — — —	35,000
Flax-Seed, 7,000 Hhds at 40 s — —	14,000
Horses, and Live Stock — — —	17,000
Timber, Plank, Masts, Boards, Staves, and Shingles	25,000
Potash, 7,000 Hhds at 40 s — —	14,000
Ships built for Sale, 20 at £ 700 —	14,000
Copper Ore, and Iron, in Bars and Pigs —	20,000
The whole at a like Average of three Years £	526,000

for ours made in Money, the most advantageous System of Trade, that can be carried on with any Country.

The flourishing State of this Province has led many to conclude that it is come to it's Meridian. But the contrary is the Fact. The same Encouragement to Agriculture, and Manufactures of the coarser and more immediately necessary Kinds, that has been proposed in the preceeding Letter to be given to *New England*, *Connecticut*, *Rhode-Island*, and *New Hampshire*, would be found to be equally beneficial to *New York*, and through that to *Great-Britain*. The Reasons which irrefragably support this Opinion are obvious in themselves, and have been so fully shewn in those Instances, that a Repetition of them cannot be necessary here. I shall therefore only observe to your Lordship, as a Proof of what this Province can produce, above its immediate Exports, that there are above 2000 Tons of Hemp and Flax, of it's own Growth, worked up there annually for it's own Use.

Nor are the Improvements of which this Province is still capable, confined to the particular Channels above-mentioned, highly advantageous as they are: The Success of repeated Experiments has proved that it abounds in valuable Metals. Iron, and Copper, have already been raised in such Quantities, as to become capital Articles of Commerce; and there can scarce be a Doubt, but other Metals, still more valuable, will also be found, when properly sought for; and so open new Sources of Trade, equally advantageous to the Colony and the Mother-Country, with whom all it's Wealth ultimately centers.

I have the Honour, &c.

LETTER XV.

My Lord,

THE adjoining Colony of *Pennsylvania* equals *New York* in all the Gifts of Nature, and perhaps exceeds it in those of Fortune, as we speak; it's Form of Civil Government being better calculated to promote private Happiness, and consequently Publick Prosperity, than any other, with which we are acquainted, under the Sun.

That this is not an Exaggeration in either Instance will appear from the following State of the Commerce of this Colony with *Great Britain*.

COMMODITIES exported from *Great Britain* to *Philadelphia*, the only Sea-port in *Pennsylvania*.

Wrought Iron, Steel, Copper, Pewter, Lead, and Brass—Birmingham, and Sheffield Wares—Hemp — Cordage— Sail-Cloth— Broad-Cloths— Colchester-Bays— Long-Ells—Stuffs—Flannels— Manchester-Goods — Hosiery, Haberdashery, and Millinery Wares—Hats—Gloves—British, Foreign, and Irish Linens—Silks—Gold, and Silver Lace—Toys—Painter's Colours—Ship-Chandlery, and Sadlery Goods — Cabinet-Wares — Earthen Wares— Grindstones— Fishing Tackle— Seeds— Pickles—Cheese—Strong-beer—Smoaking Pipes— Snuffs—Wines—Spirits, and Drugs, all which cost at an Average of three Years — } £ 611,000

The Nature of these Exports from this Colony shews that almost the whole of them is carried to other Markets, beside *Great Britain*, and consequently the Returns, for ours, are made in the Money for which these are sold there; a Circumstance, the Advantage resulting from which, as well as from the Amount of our own Exports in this Trade, has been observed in the Letter preceding this.

As

Commodities exported from *Philadelphia* to *Great Britain*, and other Markets.

Biscuit Flour, 350,000 Barrels, at 20 s	£ 350,000
Wheat, 100,000 Quarters, at 20 s	100,000
Beans—Peas—Oats—Indian Corn, and other Grain	12,000
Salt-Beef—Pork—Bacon—Hams—Venison	45,000
Bees-Wax, 20,000 lb at 1 s.	1,000
Butter—Cheese, and Tongues	10,000
Deer, and sundry other Sorts of Skins	50,000
Live Stock, and Horses	20,000
Flax-Seed, 15,000 Hhds at 40 s	30,000
Timber—Plank—Masts—Boards—Staves, and Shingles	35,000
Ships built for Sale, 25 at £ 700	17,500
Copper-Ore, and Iron in Pigs and Bars	35,000
The whole at an Average of three Years	£ 705,500

As this Colony is in every Respect circumstanced in the same Manner as *New York*, it is capable of equal Improvement by the same Means, a Repetition of which cannot be necessary here.

The Province of *New Jersey* is situated immediately next to *New York*, and *Pennsylvania*, and yields to neither in the Blessings

Bleſſings of Nature, but in other Circumſtances is yet far behind them.

The Produce of this Country is in every Inſtance the ſame with that of the others, as is it's Trade; both of which are capable of much greater Improvements than the former, for this Reaſon, that they are not yet nearly ſo much improved.

The Cauſe of this Backwardneſs though being no other than the Impoſſibility of attending to too many Things at one Time, it is to be hoped that it will ſoon ceaſe; and *New Jerſey*, from the Example of it's Neighbouring Countries, perhaps from the Spreading of their Inhabitants, as the Means of Improvement are the ſame, riſe to that Figure in itſelf, and Importance to *Great Britain*, for which it is ſo well and abundantly qualified.

The Trade of this Province being at preſent carried on ſolely with and from *New York* and *Pennſylvania*, though it wants not good and convenient Ports of it's own, is inſeperably included, both inwards and outwards, with theirs, to which it makes no inconſiderable Addition, eſpecially in the valuable Article of Copper-Ore, the greater Part of which, exported by them, is raiſed here.

I have the Honour, &c.

LETTER XVI.

My Lord,

FROM *New Jersey* we come to *Virginia* and *Maryland*, two Colonies in all Respects circumstanced so exactly alike by Nature, and so inexplicably connected with each other in Trade and Intercouse, that though politically divided into distinct Governments, they are in themselves to be considered rather as Parts of one, than as different Countries, any Attempt at drawing a Line between them in the Scale of their Commerce, being much more difficult to execute, than the Execution of it would be advantageous.

I shall therefore lay before your Lordship a State of their Trade, as it is jointly carried on by them at present, without entering here into any other Specification of their Produce, or Proof of their natural Aptitude for still farther Improvement.

Commodities exported from *Great Britain* to *Virginia* and *Maryland*.

Wrought Iron, Steel, Copper, Pewter, Lead, and Brass — *Hemp* — *Cordage* — *Sail-Cloth* — *Broad-Cloths* — *Stuffs* — *Flannels* — *Colchester-Bays* — *Long-Ells* — *British, Irish, and Foreign Linens* — *Silks* — *Gold, and Silver Lace* — *Toys* — *Millinery, Haberdashery, and Hosiery Goods* — *Hats* — *Gloves* — *Birmingham, and Sheffield Wares* — *Upholstery, Cabinet, Ship-Chandlery, and Sadlery Wares* — *Earthen Wares* — *Grindstones* — *Painter's Colours* — *Pickles* — *Seeds* — *Fishing Tackle* — *Cheese* — *Strong-beer* — *Smoking Pipes* — *Snuffs* — *Wines* — *Spirits, and Medicinal Drugs*, all which cost at an Average of three Years — — } £ 865,000

The first Thing that strikes the View, in this State of the Trade of these Provinces, is the Balance that appears upon the Face of it, against *Great Britain*. But this, as hath been observed in other Instances, is only in Appearance. All the Articles exported from *Great Britain* to *Virginia*, and *Maryland*, are of our own Produce and Manufacture, except a very few; and these also are of our own Importation, in the most lucrative Channels of our Trade; so that our Profit upon them bears a near Proportion to, if it does not equal their

Commodities exported from *Virginia* and *Maryland* to *Great Britain*, and other Markets.

Tobacco, 96,000 Hhds at £8	£768,000
Indian-Corn—Beans—Peas, &c.	30,000
Wheat, 40,000 Quarters, at 20 s	40,000
Deer, and other Skins	25,000
Iron, in Bars and Pigs	35,000
Masts—Plank—Staves—Turpentine, and Tar	55,000
Sassafras—Snake-root—Ginseng, &c.	7,000
Flax-Seed, 7,000 Hhds at 40 s	14,000
Pickled Pork—Beef—Hams, and Bacon	15,000
Ships built for Sale, 30 at £1,000	30,000
* *Hemp*, 1,000 Tons, at £21	21,000

The whole at a like Average of three Years £1,040,000

---

their first Cost to us: Whereas, not an inconsiderable Part of the Exports of *Virginia* and *Maryland*, goes to the neighbouring Colonies, in Exchange for Articles of their Produce, with which we could not supply them, but at second hand, and consequently so much dearer, that it would be equally absurd and oppressive, to expect they should take them from us.

But

* Beside this Quantity of Hemp exported raw to *Great Britain*, they raise 2,000 Tons more, and 2,000 Tons of Flax, which they work up at home for their own Use.

But this is far from being the Circumstance of most Advantage in the Trade of these Provinces. The capital Article of their Produce is Tobacco, a Commodity, which, exclusive of the private Profits of Trade to the Merchant, yields immediately to the Publick a Revenue greater than any other, in the whole Circle of our Commerce.

To prove this, I must beg leave to observe to your Lordship, that of the 96,000 Hhds of Tobacco imported annually into *Great Britain* from *Virginia* and *Maryland*, only 13,500 Hhds are consumed at home, the Duty paid by which, at the Rate of £ 26 1 0 per Hhd, amounts to £ 351,675; the remaining 82,500 Hhds being exported by our Merchants to the other Parts of *Europe*, and their Value returned to *Great Britain*.

It must be unnecessary to enter into a Detail or Proof of the Advantages arising from such a Trade, which from the Overflowing of a *Non-necessary*, keeps in our Hands a Balance against those *Necessaries*, which we are obliged to purchase from other Countries, indispensibly, and therefore at a Loss. They prove themselves on the bare Mention of them. I shall therefore only add, that this single Trade gives constant Employment to 330 Sail of Ships, and 3,960 Sailors, to shew that it's Advantages are not confined only to our Wealth, but extend to the most essential Part of our National Strength also.

It it natural to think that Advantages so obvious, and so great, have not been neglected. The Truth is, the Cultivation

tion of this Commodity has been carried as far as it will bear, there not being Vent for any greater Quantity than is now raised. But this does not preclude these Provinces from Improvement in other Instances. Attention to their Tobacco has made them in a great Measure neglect the Tillage of Corn, and be too remiss even in the Articles of Hemp and Flax, for all which they are most happily situated. To these they should be encouraged to apply themselves with Spirit, as also to the Manufactures of most immediate Necessity to them, and least Profit to the Importer from other Countries.

The Evils indeed arising from the Neglect of these indispensibly necessary Articles, at length begin to be perceived by the People of these Colonies, who have accordingly made some weak Efforts in Agriculture to raise the Corn necessary for their own Subsistence, and free themselves from the Expence and Danger of depending for their daily Bread upon other Countries, when put so bountifully within their reach by Heaven. But the Attempts of Individuals are liable to too many Interruptions; and at the best will advance too slowly to remedy an Evil, that has taken so deep Root, if they are not both encouraged and assisted by publick Munificence.

I presume not, my Lord, to direct the Manner in which this is to be done. The bare Hint is all that can come with Propriety from me to your Lordship; nor is it to be doubted, but those to whom his Majesty has delegated the Care, will with the Example of our Tillage-Act before their Eyes, soon

see

see the Expediency of what is here suggested, and apply the most effectual Measures for carrying it happily into Execution.

The Benefits which must necessarily arise from this Policy have been shewn in the former Instances, in which it has been recommended. To what has been there said, I shall not trespass upon your Lordship with any further Addition, than that in the Case of these Provinces, it seems in some Measure more immediately necessary, than in any other, the Want of a Variety of internal Employment having weakened the Spirit of Industry, and of course introduced a Turn to Dissipation and Expence in the Inhabitants, of all Degrees, that must instantly affect, and if not corrected, in Course of Time totally overturn the Prosperity of any Country.

I have the Honour, &c.

LETTER XVII.

MY LORD,

NEXT to *Virginia* and *Maryland*, lie the two Provinces of *North*, and *South Carolina*. The almost total Neglect, under which the former of these Provinces lay, till very lately; and the very little Advances made even yet, in the Improvement of it, can be accounted for only from this Observation, that the first Settlement of Countries is directed by Chance, much more than by Choice; and that even where such Choice can be made, all Things cannot be attended to, at one Time. Well it is, that our Eyes are at length opened to Advantages, which Blindness only could overlook; and that Leisure begins to be found to improve a Country, whose Soil and Climate court Cultivation with Assurances of the most grateful Returns.

Under such Disadvantages, it cannot be expected that the (I had almost said infant) Trade of this Province, can have arisen to any considerable Height. The following Account shews it in it's present State. What it may be improved to shall be considered after.

Commodities exported from *Great-Britain* to *North Carolina*.

Wrought-Iron, Steel, Copper, Lead, Pewter, and Brass—Birmingham, and Sheffield Wares—Hemp—Cordage—Sail-Cloth—Broad-Cloths—Stuffs—Flannels—Colchester Bays, and Long Ells—Sadlery—Haberdashery—Millinery, and Hosiery Goods—Hatts—Gloves—Gold and Silver Lace—Silks—British, Irish, and Foreign Linens—Upholstery, and Cabinet-Wares—Earthen-Wares—Grindstones—Fishing-Tackle—Garden-Seeds—Toys—Cheese—Pickles—Strong-Beer—Smoaking-Pipes—Snuffs—Wines—Spirits—Medicinal Drugs— All which cost at an Average of three Years — — — — } £18,000

The Excess of the Exports of this Province over it's Imports from *Great Britain*, is to be accounted for in the same Manner, as the like Excess has been in other Instances. Much the greater Part goes to the neighbouring Colonies, in Exchange for Commodities of their Produce, so that the Balance upon the whole is in Favour of *Great Britain*.

But no Judgement can justly be formed of the Value of this Province from the present Amount of it's Trade, as

hath

COMMODITIES exported from *North Carolina* to *Great-Britain*, and other Markets.

Rice, 2000 Barrels, at 40 s	£ 4,000
Tobacco, 2000 Hhds at £ 7	14,000
Pitch, Tar, and Turpentine, 51,000 Barrels, at 7 s	17,850
Boards, Staves, *Joists*, *Shingles*, *Masts*, *and Lumber*	15,000
Indian Corn, Peas, and other Grain	7,000
Live Stock of different Kinds	5,000
Skins of different Kinds	5,500
The whole at an Average of three Years	£ 68,350

hath been observed before. Every Article of it's Produce might be pushed to many Times the Quantity it is now at; and many new Articles introduced with a Certainty of Success, were the Advantages of Nature properly pursued. Pitch, &c. and Rice, are the only Commodities which *North-Carolina* now sends to *Europe*. The two former must necessarily increase, with the Encrease of Inhabitants, from the Clearing of the Country, as the Settlements are extended; and the Certainty of a good Market will encourage the Cultivation of the latter, as an Article of Commerce, as well as for Home-Consumption.

The most obvious of the new Articles, which may be introduced into the Trade of this Province, are *Corn* and *Wine*. No Argument can be wanted to enforce the Cultivation of these *first Necessaries*, if not *Indispensibles* of Life, wherever Nature will allow it. *Bread* (made of Corn) is " *the Staff of Life :* " and " *Wine maketh glad the Heart of Man.*"— All therefore that can be necessary for the present Purpose is to prove, that this Country is not improper for their Production.

And in this, my Lord, I have the Advantage of having Reason supported by Experience. The Appearance of the Soil, and Temperature of the Climate soon tempted the *European* Settlers to try the Growth of Corn in various Parts of this Country, in every one of which the Success has invariably answered their most sanguine Expectations. But they have gone but little, or no further. Satisfied with the Experiment, or unable to pursue it, at least with any View to Commerce, they go on in the beaten Path, turning their Backs to an Advantage so obvious, and so great. That such Advantage must really arise from the Culture of Corn for Exportation, will sufficiently appear from this single Consideration; that this is the last of the *British* Provinces, to the Southward, that will produce Corn; and consequently that it can supply the more Southern Colonies, at a cheaper Rate, than those at a greater Distance.

Though

Though the Experiments hitherto made for the Culture of the Vine, have not, for obvious Reasons, been so many, nor so extensive as the former, the Success has been abundantly sufficient to encourage the Pursuit of them; and scarce leaves a Doubt but this Country is capable of producing the Wines of *Switzerland*, *Germany*, and *France*, in Quantities sufficient to supply all our Colonies, and of such Quality, as perhaps in Time to tempt the Mother-Country to give it a Share of that Trade with her, in those Articles, which is now wholly in the Hands of Strangers.

The Advantages, which must result from this, are in a Manner self-evident. Wine is in such universal Use, that the Countries which cannot produce, must purchase it; as the Want of it will not be dispensed with by any.

That the Climate and Soil of *Great Britain* will not bring the Grape to such Perfection as to make it's Juice in Request, either for Health or Pleasure, has been long known! That the Climate, and Soil of several of our Southern Provinces in *America*, beginning at this of *North Carolina*, will, has been sufficiently proved by Experience! Why we should not then encourage our own Subjects to produce a Sufficiency of it, not only for their own Use, but also to supply us, and so give the Profits of the Trade to them, from whom it will return ultimately to ourselves, rather than to other Nations, cannot be reconciled with any Principles of common Prudence, much less of sound Policy.

I have mentioned only these two Articles, my Lord, not as all which may be added to the Commercial Stock of this Province, but as the moſt obvious, and eaſieſt to ſucced in; and becauſe I would not diſtract the Attention, by propoſing too many Objects at once. In the Purſuit of theſe, many others will naturally open themſelves, in Circumſtances which will beſt point out the proper Methods of purſuing them alſo; and theſe I have only juſt touched upon here, as I ſhall have Occaſion to purſue the Subject in other Inſtances.

I have the Honour, &c.

LETTER XVIII.

My Lord,

IN the Complaint of Neglect made by *North-Carolina*, the next Province of *South-Carolina* has no right to join in any Sense. Of all the *British* Colonies in *America*, this has been cultivated with most Attention, Spirit, and Expence; and the Success has been answerable. The Country is well peopled; and wears a Face of Improvement and Civilization, scarce inferior to any Part of *Europe*. It's aboriginal Products are cultivated with proper Care; and the Products of other Countries introduced, and carried nearer to the Perfection of their Nature, than Exoticks in any other Country we know.

The Advantages derived from this flourishing Colony (by the Mother Country) will appear from the following State of it's Trade.

COMMODITIES exported from *Great-Britain* to *South-Carolina*.

Wrought-Iron, Steel, Copper, Pewter, Brass and Lead — Birmingham and Sheffield Wares — Hemp — Cordage — Sail-Cloth — Broad-Cloths — Stuffs — Flannels — Colchester-Bays — Long-Ells — Sadlery — Haberdashery — Millenery — and Hosiery Goods — Hats — Gloves — Gold and Silver Lace — Silks — British, Irish, and Foreign-Linens — Upholstery, and Cabinet-Wares — Earthen Wares — Grindstones — Toys — Garden-Seeds — Cheese — Pickles — Strong Beer — Smoking-pipes — Snuffs — Wines — Medicinal Drugs — All which cost at an Average of three Years - - - } £ 365,000

The high Amount, and Nature of the Exports from *Great Britain* to this Colony (all consisting of it's own Produce and immediate Manufactures) shew the Importance of it: The Excess of the Exports of *South-Carolina* over these Imports, is to be accounted for in the same Manner, as the like Excess has been in other Instances. What Improvements this Country, and of Course, it's Trade, is still capable of, comes now to be considered.

The

Commodities exported from *South-Carolina*, to *Great-Britain*, and other Markets.

	£	s	d
Rice, 110,000 Barrels, at 40 s	220,000	0	0
Pitch, Tar, and Turpentine, 8,000 Barrels, at 6 s 8 d	2,666	13	4
Pickled Pork, and Beef	25,000	0	0
Deer and other Skins	45,000	0	0
Indigo, 500,000 lb. at 2 s	50,000	0	0
Boards, Masts, Staves, Joists, &c.	20,000	0	0
Indian-Corn, Peas, Beans, and Callivances	12,000	0	0
Live Stock and Sundries	15,000	0	0
Ships built for Sale, 10 at £ 600	6,000	0	0
The whole at an Average of three Years	£ 395,666	13	4

The favourable Representation which I have made of this Province to your Lordship, must not be applied indiscriminately to the Whole, nor taken to preclude all Necessity of farther Improvements of it.

The first Settlements being naturally made as near as possible to the Sea; the Improvements of the Country of Course begun there: But though they have been extended from thence a great Way inwards, there still remains a much greater Extent unimproved, at least comparatively to what it is capable of.

In Praise of the Spirit and Industry of the Inhabitants, and for the Encouragement of their Successors to follow so laudable an Example, it is proper to be observed, that by much the greater Part where the Improvements above-mentioned have been so successfully made, was not only the most difficult to work upon, but also the least qualified by Nature to make a suitable Return, the Country adjoining to the Sea, and from thence near eighty Miles inwards, being mostly a dead Flat, and of a light, shallow, sandy Soil; though a late Discovery has shewn that this very Soil is in a peculiar Manner adapted to produce one of the most valuable Articles of Commerce.

But from the Commencement of the Hilly Country to the Extremity of the Province, Heaven has bestowed it's Blessings with a most bounteous Hand. The Air is infinitely more temperate, and healthful, than nearer to the Sea. The Hills are covered with valuable Woods! The Vallies watered with beautiful Rivers! and the Fertility of the Soil is equal to every vegetable Production. All that remains therefore is to turn these Blessings to our best Advantage.

From the foregoing State of the Exports of this Country, it appears that the capital Article of it's Production is Rice. Great as the Quantity already raised of this is, a still greater might be raised, to answer any new Demand. The Quantities of Skins, and Pitch, &c. would necessarily increase with
the

the Settlement of the back Country. The Importance of *Indigo*, the Produce of the sandy Soil hinted at above, is already too well known, to require any Illustration, or Argument to urge Attention to it.

The only new Article, both of Commerce and Home-consumption, obviously and immediately necessary to be introduced into the Stock of this Country is *Wine*. The Expediency of making this, wherever Nature will allow it, has been sufficiently shewn in the preceding Instance of *North-Carolina*. To what has been there advanced, it is sufficient to add, in the present Case, that *South-Carolina* has been proved by repeated Experiments, to be capable of producing the same Wines of *Switzerland*, *Germany*, *France*, and *Portugal* as her more Northern Sister, and that too with an equal, at least, if not a greater Degree of Perfection.

I am aware that there is another Article, of which some Experiments have been made, and speculative Men talked much, as capable of being cultivated with Advantage in this Colony. This is *Silk*. The Importance of such an Addition to the Trade of any Country requires no Proof. The only Question is, whether that Importance, great as it is, may not be purchased at too high a Price. The Thinness of Population, in all our Colonies, makes every Article, that requires many Hands, come so dear, that it is found better to import than make them. Add to this, that our next Colony of *Georgia* is in every Respect much better adapted to the Production of this valuable Article, than *South-Carolina*. Let us then confine the Cultivation of it to the latter, and not, by seeking more than we can compass, run the Hazard of neglecting what is in our Power, and so losing the Substance to grasp at the Shadow.

The same may be said with Respect to *Cotton*, which, though possible to be produced here, is yet the natural Produce of the more Southern Colonies, from whence it may, of Course, be had with more Advantage.

I have not, my Lord, said any Thing of the Probability of discovering valuable Mines, in either of the Colonies of *North* or *South-Carolina*, for several Reasons. Where the certain Advantages are sufficiently great, it is unnecessary, if not dangerous, to propose such as are doubtful to the Pursuit. Beside, that I really think the Riches earned by gradual Industry are in their Consequences infinitely more valuable, than those which come upon us, as it were, in an accidental Shower.

I have the Honour, &c.

LETTER XIX.

My Lord,

OUR next Province, to the Southward of the *Carolinas*, is *Georgia*. Though the Neceffity of eftablifhing a Barrier between our's, and the *Spanifh* Colonies, the firft Motive for forming a Settlement in this Country, has been removed by the Ceffion of the *Floridas* to *Great Britain*, the Attempt has opened other Advantages of Weight abundantly fufficient to determine us not to relinquifh the Undertaking, the Soil and Climate being found to be particularly proper for the Production of fome moft valuable Commodities, which our other Colonies cannot produce in equal Perfection, nor at all without much more Labour and Expence.

But before I enter into an Inveftigation of what this Country is capable of producing, I fhall firft lay before your Lordfhip a State of it's prefent Trade, according to the Plan I have purfued, through the Courfe of this Undertaking.

COMMODITIES exported from *Great Britain* to *Georgia*.

Wrought Iron, Steel, Copper, Pewter, Lead, and Brass—Birmingham, and Sheffield Wares—Hemp—Cordage—Sail-Cloth—Broad-Cloths—Stuffs—Flannels—Colchester-Bays—Long-Ells—Sadlery—Haberdashery—Millinery—and Hosiery Goods—Hats—Gloves—Gold, and Silver Lace—Silks—British, Irish, and Foreign Linens—Earthen Ware—Grindstones—Fishing Tackle—Painter's Colours—Ship-Chandlery Goods—Manchester Goods—Upholstery, and Cabinet Wares—Stationary Wares—Books—Toys—Garden Seeds—Smoking Pipes—Snuffs—Strong-beer—Wines—Medicinal Drugs, all which cost at an Average of three Years } £ 49,000

Inconsiderable as the Amount of this may at first View appear, yet when the very late Establishment of the Colony, and the very many Difficulties it has had to struggle with, are taken into the Consideration, it will appear more worthy of Remark, that it should have risen so high. The Reason of the Excess of it's Exports over it's Imports has been already explained in similar Instances.

The

Commodities exported from *Georgia*, to *Great Britain*, and other Markets.

Rice, 18,000 Barrels, at 40 s	£ 36,000
Indigo, 17,000 lb. at 2 s	1,700
Silk, 2,500 lb. at 20 s	2,500
Deer, and other Skins	17,000
Boards, Staves, &c.	11,000
Tortoise-Shell, Drugs, Cattle, and Live Stock, &c.	6,000
The whole at a like Average of three Years	£ 74,200

The capital Articles in the present Trade of *Georgia*, are Rice, Indigo, and Skins; every one of which may, and most probably will, for the Reasons given in the preceding Instances of the *Carolinas*, be pushed to many Times the above Amount, as the Settlement of the Country shall be extended.

But the Importance of this Province is not rested on these Articles alone, important as they evidently are. In Addition to them, others of equal, perhaps greater Weight in the Scale

of

of Commerce, may be introduced.   Thefe are *Wine*, and *Silk*.

The Expediency, I may almoft fay Neceffity, of cultivating the Vine, wherever it can be brought to Perfection, has been already fhewn. To what has been there laid down, it it fufficient to add in the prefent Inftance, that this Province of *Georgia*, has been proved by Experience to be in every Refpect proper for producing the Wines of *Portugal*, *Spain*, *Italy*, *Madeira*, and the *Canaries*, of Quality at leaft not inferiour to what we purchafe from thefe Countries, and in Quantities equal to our Demand for them.

The National Advantages which muft neceffarily refult from bringing home fuch a Trade to ourfelves, from the Hands of Foreign Nations, are felf-evident. I fhall therefore fay no more on the Occafion, than that if the Conduct of the Firft of the Countries above-mentioned, from whence we are now chiefly fupplied with Wine for our Home-Confumption, for fome Years paft, is adverted to, indignant and juft Refentment will enforce the Purfuit of fuch a Meafure.

The Arguments adduced in the Cafe of *Wine*, may, in a great Degree, be applied to *Silk*. Ufe has brought it to be reckoned almoft a Neceffary of Life. At leaft the Want of it will not be difpenfed with by thofe who can poffibly purchafe it, at any Price. The Production of this Article therefore, if only in Quantity fufficient for our own Ufe, muft be an important Saving; if fufficient to be introduced into foreign Trade, a moft important Addition to the publick Stock.

The

The Climate of *Georgia* has been found to agree in every Respect with the Silk-Worm; the Vegetables, which are it's natural Food, are indigenous to it; and the Silk, that has been produced there, has proved equal in Quality to the best, that can be purchased any where. The only Obstacle then that appears to oppose the Pursuit of so advantageous an Object, is the Want of a sufficient Number of Hands to prepare it in such a Quantity as may deserve publick Attention. But even this Obstacle lessens, when taken into nearer Consideration.

The only Hands, required to fit the Work of the Silk-Worm for Trade, are those of Women, and Children, before they arrive at Age and Strength for more laborious Occupations. That the Application of these to this Branch will not interfere with any other that can be of publick Concern, is obvious; as it is also a known Fact, that the Number of People encreases in Proportion to the Encrease of the Support which they can earn by their Industry. While the Men therefore turn their Attention and Time to such Business, as they only can execute, that Part of their Families, which would otherwise be a Burden upon their Industry, and keep them in continual Want, and Depressure of Spirits, will, by the Means here proposed, reverse the whole Scene, filling their Habitations with Plenty, and their Hearts with Gladness, the true, and never-failing Sources of Population. That this is not visionary Speculation, and that this Trade is capable of producing the Effects here ascribed to it, appears in all the Countries, where it is pursued, which though labouring under many Difficulties, and Discouragements unknown in the

Dominions

Dominions of *Great Britain*, are still full of an healthy and chearful People.

I have thus, my Lord, endeavoured to point out the Advantages, which may be reaped from this, till very lately neglected Country. That in the Pursuit of these many others may open themselves, is more than probable. But I have religiously adhered to the Principle laid down at my Entrance upon this Undertaking, to advance nothing upon meer Conjecture, or which I cannot vouch upon my own Experience.

There are other Particulars, beside what immediately relates to the Produce and Trade of this Colony, which in their Consequences must affect them, and therefore well deserve Attention. But I shall reserve these for another Letter, as they are applicable also to the Country which comes next under Consideration; and this is already swelled to too great a Length.

I have the Honour, &c.

LETTER XX.

My Lord,

WE are at length arrived at *Florida*, the Boundary of the *British* Empire, and consequently the End of our Travels on the Continent of *America*. A new Acquisition of Territory is always the Subject of much Speculation, and Controversy. This of *Florida* has been so much, and so contrarily described, since it came into our Possession, that a Word on either Side of the Question is sure of meeting Contradiction. In such Cases, the middle Way is generally held to be the safest; in this it is certainly the right; the Advantages and Disadvantages, the Praise and Dispraise of this Country being equally exaggerated, in every Particular, and that from the same Motive of Self-interest. This will appear when it is considered who the Persons are, who have given such Descriptions.

The People, who have obtained Grants of Lands in *Florida*, and want to settle or sell them, represent the whole Country as a *Canaan*, "flowing with Milk and Honey," in order to tempt Purchasers, or allure Adventurers to go thither with them. The Army, who have been sent there to take and keep the Possession, exclaim against it as an *Aceldama*, "a Field of Blood," designed to be the burying Place of all Strangers, who are so unhappy as to go there.

Contradictory as these Representations are, it is not so difficult, as it may appear, to reconcile them. The Sea-coasts, where the Fortresses, judged necessary for protecting the Navigation, and maintaining the Possession, have been erected, are barren, and unhealthy, in an extream Degree. The inland Country, from the Commencement of the Hills, is healthful, and not only fertile in all it's aboriginal Productions; but also fit to produce many exotick to it, in the highest Perfection. All necessary therefore to decide between the different Characters, drawn with equal Warmth and Confidence of Assertion, of *Florida*, is to distinguish between those two Parts of it, and give to each it's own. The Consequence in respect to the former is obvious. Of the latter, it is not mine to judge: All that comes within my Province, being to point out the Advantages, in a commercial View, which this Country is capable of producing to *Great Britain*.

Florida is divided, like *Carolina*, into two Provinces of the same Name, and distinguished only by their Situation on the *Eastern*, or *Western* Sides of the Country.

Most of the Disadvantages, indiscriminately imputed to the whole Country, should be confined to *East Florida*, which is for the greater Part, a flat, sandy, and almost barren Desert. The most considerable Fortress and Port for Trade in this Province is *St. Augustine*.

It is not to be expected, that a Settlement so new, and under such Circumstances, can have yet made any very considerable Advances in Trade. Our Exports to *St. Augustine* consist of the same Commodities, as those to the neighbouring

ing Provinces of *Georgia* and *Carolina*, and amount to about £7,000 annually. Imports from thence, we have yet received none worth bringing to Account.

It must not be concluded from hence though, that the Country is incapable of producing any Commodities proper for Exportation; or that it may not be brought to take off much greater Quantities of ours, than it does at present. The Contrary is the Fact, in both Instances. With proper Cultivation it will produce Rice, Indigo, Silk, Wines, and Cochineal, so as to be brought into Commerce on advantageous Terms. The Importance of these Articles requires no Proof. The last in particular will be one of the most advantageous Additions, that can be made to our commercial Stock, as it enters deeply into the Manufacturing of some of our most valuable Commodities, for which Purpose we are now obliged to purchase it from others, at what Price they please to impose; whereas if we produce it ourselves, we shall not only save the greater Part of that Price, and thereby be enabled to carry those Manufactures to Market on cheaper Terms, than we can at present; but also to turn the Scales, and set our own Price upon it to other Countries.

The Importance of this Colony though arises not from the immediate Produce of this or any other Article, however important in itself; but from the Advantage of it's Situation, indeed of the whole Country of *Florida*, for carrying on a Trade with the *Spanish* Colonies; it being certain that a regular Intercourse might be established with them, which would open a Vent for the Commodities of *Great Britain*, and yield Returns for them in Gold and Silver, the moſt profitable of all Kinds of Commerce, to an Amount ſuperiour to any Trade we have.

I have the Honour, &c.

LETTER XXI.

My Lord,

AS the Diſadvantages under which *Eaſt Florida* has been ſhewn to labour, extend not to it's Siſter Province of *Weſt Florida*, the latter conſequently adds the Importance of internal Produce, and Aptitude for Population, to that of peculiar Situation for Trade with the *Spaniſh* Colonies, in which, as hath been obſerved before, it ſhares equally with it; there not being perhaps on the whole Continent of *America*, any Place better qualified by Nature to afford not only all the Neceſſaries of Life, but alſo all the Pleaſures of Habitation, than that Part of this Country, which lies upon the Banks of the *Miſſiſſipi*.

Of this Difference between theſe two Provinces, the different Amount of their reſpective Trades, occaſioned by the Difference between their Population, is the beſt Proof.

Com-

COMMODITIES exported from *Great-Britain* to *Pensacola*, the Capital of *West Florida*.

Wrought-Iron, Steel, Copper, Pewter, Brass and Lead — Birmingham and Sheffield Wares — Hemp — Cordage — Sail-Cloth — Broad-Cloths — Stuffs — Flannels — Colchester-Bays — Long-Ells — Manchester Goods — Hosiery — Haberdashery — and Millenery Goods — Gloves — Hats — British, Irish, and Foreign Linens — Gold and Silver Lace — Silks — India Goods — Cabinet — Upholstery — and Ship-Chandlery Wares — Painter's Colours — Pictures — Books — Stationary Wares — Earthen Wares — Grindstones — Toys — Smoaking-pipes — Cheese — Strong Beer — Wines — Pickles — Snuffs — all which cost at an Average of three Years — — } £ 97,000

The COMMODITIES exported from *Pensacola* to *Great-Britain*, are

Skins — Logwood — and other dying Woods — and Silver in Dollars — amounting annually to } £ 63,000

The Infancy of the Colony will sufficiently account for the Fewness of the Articles in the above List of Exports; as it it will also for the Balance against them in Value; the Surplus being indispensibly necessary to effect the Settlement, and keep a Stock in Hand for the *Spanish* Trade, till a sufficient Fund shall be established for that Purpose.

Beside the Articles here enumerated, *West Florida* yields all the West-Indian Produce naturally; and is also capable of producing many of the most valuable Articles of other Countries, particularly Medicinal Druggs of several Kinds, Wines, Indigo, and Cochineal, all of which are of such known Importance in Commerce, that no Argument can be necessary to enforce the Cultivation of them.

A Country so rich in commercial Produce, and so happily situated for the richest Species of foreign Commerce, cannot want People. It's Advantages only want to be known to draw Men of Enterprize and Genius from every other Country to the Harvest, especially under the Protection of such a Government as that of *Great Britain*, which ensures the free Enjoyment of their Acquisitions to them; and so makes every Son of Freedom it's own.

In what I had the Honour to suggest to your Lordship concerning the Province of *Georgia*, I mentioned reserving some farther Hints to another Place. This, my Lord, is the Place I meant.

It has been observed, that the original Motive of *Great Britain* for settling *Georgia*, was to establish a Barrier between

our

our other Colonies, particularly the *Carolinas*, and the *Spaniards* and their *Indians*, in *Florida*.

The Acquisition of *Florida*, instead of taking away, has in reality heightened the Necessity of such a Barrier, by changing the Place of it; as it is evident, that the *Spaniards* will be doubly jealous of a Colony, advanced so much nearer to their's, and situated so conveniently for a Trade with them, that counteracts a fundamental Principle of their Government, that of keeping the Supply of their *American* Dominions with *European* Commodities entirely in their own Hands.

That a military Force, and Fortresses, or Places of Arms are indispensibly necessary for the Purpose of protecting a Country that lies open to the Inroads of Enemies is evident; but though they may be the first, they are by no Means the only Necessaries in the present Instance; where the *Indians*, the Enemies principally to be guarded against, act entirely by Surprize, invading in small Parties like Robbers, murdering the People, and destroying all the Effects which they cannot carry off.

The Inefficacy of Forts, and the Inability of *European* Soldiers to protect a Country from such Ravagers, have been shewn in former * Instances; and the † Remedy proper to be applied in the present Instance, pointed out. Against the *Indians*, while Enemies, there is no Safety. They must
be

* *Page* 53.   † *Pages* 25 and 26.

be made Friends, to make their Neighbours safe. Nor is this difficult. In their natural Dispositions they are brave, honest, generous, and friendly; and as grateful for Benefits, as revengeful of Injuries. Honest, generous, and friendly Treatment will therefore evidently win them to our Interest; and this the more readily, as they know the Difference between it, and that of the *Spaniards*, whose Oppressions and Cruelties they have a most lively and indelible Sense of; and will eagerly, and cordially connect themselves with those, who shall not only use them better; but also give them a Prospect of Protection and Assistance, whenever Occasion may offer for their gratifying their darling Passion of Revenge.

I mean not by this, my Lord, to stimulate these uninformed People, to Acts of Violence against others, which we complain of ourselves. I only shew how we may avert this Violence from our own Heads, so effectually as even to turn it against those of our Enemies, if we should be authorized by Necessity so to do.

Nor is this the only Advantage, to be proposed with moral Certainty of Success, from such a Conduct towards the native Indians. They would soon learn our Manners, and, incorporating themselves with us, become a Part of our own People; I will confidently say, a most useful Part, as they would take that Labour upon them, which from the Difference of Climates, we are unequal to; and so free us from the Necessity, and Danger of importing the untractable Negroes of *Africa*, whose Numbers hourly threaten the Safety of our

Colonies

Colonies, as their Expence is an heavy Burthen upon their Trade.

I shall not enter here into the Advantages, and Duty of informing these Indians in the *Christian* Religion; as it will properly come into another Place, where the Application will be more general.

I have the Honour, &c.

LETTER XXII.

My Lord,

HAVING thus ran down the whole Length of the *British* Empire, on the Continent of *America*, I shall beg your Lordship's Leave to stop here for a Moment, and cast a Look back, over the immense Regions we have traversed.

At our setting out on this Journey, I said it was the mutual Interest of *Britain* and her Colonies, to preserve Harmony, and good Agreement with each other. To prove the first Part of this Position, *The Interest of Britain*, I have distinctly

distinctly and faithfully shewn the great Advantages, which at present are, and the greater which yet may be received by her from these her thriving Children. The Advantages reciprocally received by the Colonies, require no Proof. They appear self-evident, from the Nature of the Connection, and Intercourse between them. Their Wants are supplied! Their Weakness is supported! They sleep in Peace, and they awake in Freedom; under the Protection of a powerful and indulgent Parent!

It will probably be remarked, that in the Course of these Observations, I have universally recommended Agriculture, and Extention of Settlement. The latter establishes itself: it being evident, that the Wealth, Strength, and Importance, of every Country are in Proportion to it's Population. As to Agriculture, however strange it may appear to those, who search no deeper than the Surface, to propose the same Thing, in so many Countries, differing so widely from each other in every Circumstance, it will be found, upon closer Enquiry, that this is essentially, and equally proper and necessary for them all.

The greatest Disadvantage possible for any Country to labour under, is not to have the indispensible Necessaries of Life within itself; not only because of the constant Danger of Delay or Miscarriage of Supplies from other Countries; but also because those Countries always have it in their Power to distress the Purchasers by imposing what Price they please upon that, the Want of which they know cannot be dispensed with. The first Thing therefore to be taken Care of in

establish-

establishing foreign Colonies, is to enable them to raise their own immediate Subsistence at Home, without being obliged to depend upon other Countries for it. Subsistence, may be said to be a Term so comprehensive as to include every Thing, that may be eaten; but in the present Case, I use it in a more limited Sense, and intend only that first Necessary of Life, *Bread*, whether made of our Corn, or of Rice, the Corn of the Southern Hemisphere; any, if not indeed all, other Kind of Food, animal or vegetable, being unnecessary, in Comparison with this.

This sufficiently proves the general and indispensible Necessity of Agriculture; a Necessity for which Heaven has made as general Provision, there not being any known Country on the Globe, which will not, with proper Cultivation, yield this Support, *this Staff of Life*. And this Necessity was so obvious, that Tillage was the first Exertion of Human Industry, and that to which the highest Honour was annexed, in the uncorrupted Simplicity of antient and true Wisdom. Nor was the Preheminence given only by Man. The Pursuit of it has ever been encouraged by Heaven above all others, with the Rewards of Health, Strength, and Increase, the first Blessings of Life.

I would not be understood by this to recommend Agriculture equally, in all Countries. Many Circumstances may vary the Degree, in which it should be pursued. Climate, Soil, Inconvenience for Exportation may clog it with so many Disadvantages, that to attempt more than acquiring a Sufficiency for immediate Subsistence would be most imprudent.

dent. Let that be amply provided every where! But let those only who can carry their Harvest to an advantageous Market, and on Terms of Advantage, go further. Plenty of Corn at home makes every Thing necessary for the Support of Life plenty, and consequently cheap; but as an Article of Commerce, too much will glut the Market, and make it of no Price: A Caution applicable also to the Fisheries on the several Coasts of *Hudson's Bay*, *Labrador*, and *Newfoundland*, &c. of the Produce of which, taken in proper Proportion, there may be found advantageous and sufficient Vent to establish their Prosperity; but if pursued too far in any one Place, it would ruin not only that, but also all the rest.

The same Restriction, my Lord, I must beg Leave to make in other Instances. In the Accounts I have given of the several Provinces, which we have reviewed, I have carefully and faithfully enumerated every Article, which I know, or have just Reason to think them capable of producing. But I do not by this recommend the Culture of every Article indiscriminately, every where. Those only, which can be produced to best Advantage would I have pursued, at least with any View to Commerce.

An Instance or two will perhaps explain this more fully.

It has been shewn, that *South Carolina* will produce Silk; and *Georgia* Cochineal. This they most certainly can do, and that to Advantage, if we had no other Places, which would produce them to greater; but as it is known that *Georgia* will produce Silk, better than *South Carolina*; and
Florida

Florida Cochineal better than *Georgia*, what an Abſurdity would it be to fly in the Face of Nature, and purſue the Cultivation of either, where ſhe has denied the Advantage. It is right to know the Extent of every Country's Produce! It is right to purſue only the moſt advantageous.

There is another Particular, my Lord, which I have juſt glanced at in one or two Inſtances, but which I am convinced is the Means moſt eſſentially neceſſary to be taken to puſh the Advantages of thoſe Colonies, to their natural Extent. This is cultivating, civilizing, chriſtianizing, if I may ſo ſay, the Natives.

The Advantages of this in a political, and the Duty in a religious Light, are equally obvious. Nor can it be attended with any Difficulty, that ſhould diſcourage the Attempt. Except in the ſingle Inſtance of *Nova Scotia*, the Diſpoſition of the native, and neighbouring *Indians* of every Country we poſſeſs, invites it. Their own Vices and Virtues are thoſe of uninformed Nature. Like a too luxuriant Soil, they want only proper Cultivation, to make the Produce uniformly good, that is, as far as the weak, unſtable Nature of Man can be ſo. This much is certain, that they have learned their greateſt Vices from us; and therefore we ſurely have no Right to upbraid them with them. For Good, they naturally return Good: as they naturally return Evil for Evil; becauſe they have not been taught otherwiſe, either by Precept or Example. Ought we then to complain if the Meaſure, with which they mete to us our own, overflows? Was their Reſpect, their Eſteem, their Affection won by good Offices, by
upright

upright and generous Dealing, they would return them an hundred-fold. They would lie down at our Feet; they would work for us by Day; and guard us by Night.

The Duty in a religious, is ſtill greater than the Advantage in a political Light, as beſide the greater Excellence of the Object, it alſo includes that Advantage. To explain this Duty, to a People profeſſing Chriſtianity, would be an Inſult either upon their Principles, or their Underſtanding. If they know it not, they have the Scriptures! If they will not believe them, " neither will they believe the Voice of one riſen from the Dead;" much leſs that of a Man coming without Power or Authority to ſpeak to them. I ſhall therefore only ſay, that to expect Advantage from any Undertaking, without firſt ſtriving to conciliate the Favour of Heaven by ſuch moſt obvious, moſt indiſpenſible Means, is to contradict the Light of Reaſon as well as of Religion, and ſlight the Experience of all Ages.

I muſt not preſume to ſay more. The Duty is ſufficiently known. The Right, the Power of enforcing it, with any Proſpect of Succeſs, is not in me.

I have the Honour, &c.

LETTER XXIII.

My Lord,

THOUGH I hope I have clearly proved by the unerring Evidence of Facts, the mutual Advantages, which *Great Britain* and her Colonies reap from each other; yet as Matter diffused over a large Space may not operate so strongly upon the Mind, as when collected together, I shall beg Leave to draw the Whole into one Point of View, and then leave Reason to form it's own Conclusion.

The first Ends proposed in planting Colonies, are to encrease the Strength of the Mother Country by providing Room for an Encrease of People; and to encrease it's Wealth by establishing with them an Intercourse of Commerce, mutually advantageous, Colonization in any other View than one of them, or tending to them, being absurd, and subversive of itself.

That our Colonies, on the Continent of *America*, will abundantly answer the first of these Purposes, has been proved by Experience, wherever the Experiment has been made; and is clear to Reason in those others, where either Want of Time, or other less justifiable Causes, have hitherto prevented the Trial in any Extent, as at *Hudson's Bay*, *Labrador*, *Nova Scotia*, &c. &c.

The

The only Objection poffible to be made to pufhing this Advantage to it's full Heighth, is the Danger of depopulating the Mother Country, on a Suppofition of it's not having People to fpare for fuch Tranfplantations: but this Suppofition, and of Courfe the Apprehenfion arifing from it, are groundlefs. The Overflowings of this Metropolis (*London*) who, for want of being properly employed, are a dead Weight upon the Induftry of thofe who are, and upon the Trade of the Nation, their unearned Confumption being the real Caufe of the Scarcity and Dearnefs of the Neceffaries of Life, which makes all our Manufactures come fo dear to Market, would afford a greater Stock to breed, than would be requifite to plant every Colony I have propofed; and confequently fending them out for that Purpofe, inftead of diftreffing the Mother Country, would double the Advantage immediately to her, by delivering her from that dead Weight, as hath been already fhewn at large *. The quick Encreafe of Population, where there is proper Encouragement, and Room for Induftry to procure Plenty, is fufficiently known.

That the fecond of thefe Ends, the Eftablifhment of an advantageous Commerce has been already anfwered by every Colony we have planted, will be proved to Conviction by the State of the refpective Trade of each. How much farther that Advantage may ftill be carried, has been repeatedly and clearly fhewn in the preceding Remarks.

* *Pages* 28 and 29.

Total

Total Amount of *British* Ships, and Seamen employed in the Trade between *Great Britain*, and her Colonies on the Continent of *America*——of the Value of Goods exported from *Great Britain* to these Colonies,—and of their Produce exported to *Great Britain* and elsewhere——

Colonies	Ships	Seamen	Exports from Great Britain	Exports from the Colonies
Hudson's Bay	4	130	£ 16,000	£ 29,340
Labrador *American Vessels* 120				49,050
Newfoundland (2000 Boats)	380	20,560	273,400	345,000
Canada	34	408	105,000	105,500
Nova Scotia	6	72	26,500	38,000
New England	46	552	395,000	370,500
Rhode-Island, Connecticut and New Hampshire	3	36	12,000	114,500
New York	30	330	531,000	526,000
Pennsylvania	35	390	611,000	705,500
Virginia and Maryland	330	3,960	865,000	1,040,000
North Carolina	34	408	18,000	68,350
South Carolina	140	1,680	365,000	395,666
Georgia	24	240	49,000	74,200
St. Augustine	2	24	7,000	
Pensacola	10	120	97,000	63,000
	1,078	28,910	3,370,900	3,924,606

Let the Addition of the above Numbers of Ships, and Seamen—The Profits upon the above Cost of the Goods exported from *Great Britain*, and upon the Value of the unmanufactured Produce of the Colonies sent in return, with the Employment given to the Manufacturers, be taken into Consideration! And then let him who will presume to say that our *American* Colonies do not pay an Equivalent for every Benefit they receive, stand forth, and prove his Assertion, by the same Evidence of Facts, as this.

Nor do I rest the Point here. I will be bold to say farther, to your Lordship, that when the Amount of the Revenue received by Government from these Exports, and the returned Produce is added to the Account, it will incontestibly appear, that instead of being a Burthen upon *Great Britain*, her Colonies do in reality lighten her Burthen, by taking fully their Proportion of it upon them.

But this, my Lord, must be reserved till we shall have continued our Progress through the *West-Indian* Islands; as attempting to divide the Revenues arising from their blended Trade and Produce would only cause Confusion, and embarrass the Question.

I have the Honour, &c.

www.ingramcontent.com/pod-product-compliance
Lightning Source LLC
Chambersburg PA
CBHW030401170426
43202CB00010B/1453